Dartmouth & Kingswear during the Second World War 1939-45

Arthur L. Clamp

The Holwill Family in Dartmouth, prepared for war, 1944
Many local families were involved in a variety of activities during the dark days of the 1940s. Here one family is in uniform showing, in the front, Mrs. Dorothy Holwill, organiser and helper at the W.V.S. canteen on the Embankment, Nelsen, the dog, runner for the H.G., and Fred C. Holwill, special constable. Top row: Denis Holwill, corporal in the Air Training Corps, Bruce Holwill, W/O R.A.F. Gunner Instructor in South Wales and George Holwill, Air Training Cadet.

This version of the book is virtually as originally published.
There are now additional pages at the back providing information about the author.

The republishing project is being managed by Arthur's grandson, Steven Gibson. We aim to find all the research that he was involved in publishing, preserving it for the next generation as part of 'The Clamp Collection'.

INTRODUCTION

This illustrated booklet has been produced on the occasion of the fiftieth anniversary of the departure of troops for the Normandy Landings in June 1944. Dartmouth and Kingswear, like many other coastal towns, played a very special part in the Second World War acting as one of the host ports to American forces deployed in the West Country in readiness for the landings in France which set the stage for the eventual collapse of Hitler's Third Reich.

Although the first half of 1944 was the most active time of the whole war for the Dartmouth area when military activity reached feverish levels planning for the departure of 435 ships of the U.S. Navy, the Dart estuary witnessed a wide variety of troops, ships and land based activities defended by guns, barrage balloons, a nearby radar station, boom defence across the estuary and a very active Civil Defence service.

Fifty years ago the Dart estuary was bustling with vessels of many descriptions, troops and navy personnel were an every day scene maintaining a watchful eye lest an attack came from sea or land. Wrens, Free French Forces, Canadian, American and other nationalities were represented in this military scenario.

The Civil Defence were equally active on both sides of the estuary through the A.R.P., special constables, fire watchers, Womens Voluntary Service and, of course, the Home Guard. There was the N.F.S. supported by the A.F.S., Army and Air Training Cadets while many local officials became responsible for billeting evacuees and service personnel, organising of first aid posts, rest centres, maintenance of the blackout, public air raid shelters, emergency provision of food and a host of other activities. Everyday matters of fuel, food and clothing rationing had to be planned, gas masks, static water tanks and emergency water supplies were also other factors.

Dartmouth with its Royal Naval College and Kingswear with its shipyard at Noss were to be prime targets for attack in this locality. There were hundreds of alerts most without any serious consequences but at least on nine occasions attacks by enemy aircraft caused a variety of damage with bombs also falling in the estuary or surrounding countryside.

There were two major raids the first on 18th September, 1942, at Noss Works and the other on 13th February, 1943, on Dartmouth itself. Both are described in this title.

The main events of the wartime years are recorded here but the following should also be noted.

There was a radar station near Kingswear at Coleton Camp set up in March, 1940, forming a link in a chain of secret radar sites along the southern coast. Early warning could be given of approaching enemy aircraft and shipping could also be monitored. Bombs fell close to it in 1942 and it was guarded by the R.A.F. Regiment. It was operational all around the clock until 1945 when it reverted to a care and maintenance status finally closing in 1949.

Nearby at Brownston was a large two gun battery operated by Coastal Defence Forces similar to one at Dartmouth Castle. Searchlights were operating from here and accommodation was in nearby nissen huts. Also near the castle was a multi-rocket gun unit manned by the Royal Artillery. Bofor guns were sited on Hoodown Hill, by the Yacht Hotel, in Coronation Park, at Noss Works and at Townstal where the *Lord Nelson* pub stands. Machine gun positions were operational along the rail embankment between the ferries.

A balloon depot was in Mayor's Avenue where repair work and replenishment of gas cylinders took place serving many sites in the area. These were not always static but were at times at Townstal, Coronation Park, Avenue Gardens, Kingswear railway sidings and on barges moored in the estuary.

A defence boom across the estuary was made up of pontoons linked together and served by a boom defence vessel moored by the castle opening and closing the boom to allow vessels in and out of the harbour. Close by below Kingswear Court was sited two torpedo tubes ready to be fired if any enemy vessel ventured into the harbour.

It is not possible to include all the events in a book of this size, this perhaps could be undertaken by someone who lived through those challenging years. For this anniversary the author hopes that the following pages show to good effect the many facets of wartime Dartmouth and Kingswear and will bring to memory many happy and sad occasions of those now distant years.

ACKNOWLEDGEMENTS AND DEDICATION

Although there are many documentary sources of information on this period the day to day scenes and events more often than not come from peoples' memories or memories jogged by looking at long forgotten photographs. This booklet is based upon many peoples' accounts and for this I wish to record my many thanks and hope these pages maybe an acceptable reflection of the dark years of the 1940s.

I wish to thank B. Penwill, R. Chase, T. Huddy, H. Hutchings, R. Jones, B. Holwill, Monsieur LeBalleur, E. Ackhurst, S. Waycott, G. Wasley, R. Caudell, G. Philip, Mr. and Mrs. F. Tremlett, Mrs. M. Macleod, D. Damerell, H. Brown, the staff of the Dartmouth Museum, especially Mrs. Cawthorne, and staffs of Plymouth and British Library, London, without whose help and encouragement this booklet would not have been completed. Many loaned photographs, small posters, etc. most being included in this title. R. and F. Little kindly provided most of the Kingswear information.

An acknowledgement is appropriate as it was through the many difficulties, deprivations and losses of family and friends that Dartmouth and Kingswear people played their part in this war. There were many references to many people who worked hard but time and again the name of Alderman W. G. Row, Mayor of Dartmouth during the war years, assisted by his wife, came to the fore and for this I include him here.

Arthur L. Clamp,
203 Elburton Road,
Plymouth, Devon PL9 8HX

Protection of Buildings and Painting White Lines

These two photographs show part of the work undertaken at Dartmouth in preparation for the war as listed on this page. This was undertaken between August and November 1939.

DARTMOUTH'S £3200 ON A.R.P. IN TWELVE WEEKS

Official Account of How Money Has Been Spent

PREPARATIONS FOR HOSTILITIES

It was becoming increasingly evident in 1938 and 1939 that war with Germany was almost inevitable and, therefore, steps were taken to set up A.R.P. Defence Services in towns throughout the country. For Dartmouth £3,200 was spent over a period of twelve weeks from August to November, 1939, setting up local units, appointing officers and buying equipment based upon directives sent down by Devon County Council.

This initial expenditure proved to be higher than expected so cuts were made to the plans but the overall result was that the town was on a good footing by the end of 1939 to cope with any wartime situation. The town defence services were reported as follows:

Report centre: Personnel of 23 with the town clerk as officer in charge. Two to be continuously on duty at cost of £6 per week.

Wardens: Permanently manned posts at Coombe Road, 5 Pathfields, Orleans, South Town, Drawing office in the Market. 8 posts to be manned in an emergency at 24 Foss Street, 5 Lower Street, 1 Fairview Road, Dean's Lodge, 9 Higherside, 2 South Ford Road and 30 Victoria Road. Women £2 and men £3 per week in wages.

Squads: Decontamination squad 10 men, Rescue and demolition 25 men under J. H. Oke, Repair squad 9 men, Water, Gas and Electricity squads have no full time men.

First Aid Parties: Two parties of 5 men. Four on full time service at £3 per week. Duties also undertaken by St. John's Ambulance Brigade.

Ambulance service: Personnel of 15 under W. H. Jefford, sanitary inspector. Eleven of this service are women.

Fire Brigade: 3 full time and 3 part time with 22 auxiliaries and 17 retained men. Both action stations have been dismanned and the equipment returned to the fire station.

Cleansing station: Tender of £630 was accepted to set this station up.

First Aid Post: Personnel 59 volunteers; instructions from County to adapt Flavel Hall which cost £251 19s. 6d.

Public shelters: Five prepared at a cost of £103 18s. (See article on shelters.)

Protection of Buildings: Nine buildings have been protected by sandbags and by other means at a cost of £138. Hospital, Report centre (Guildhall), Warden's post at Market Square, Fire station and Coombe chlorination plant. Also Girls' school, Infants' school, Catholic school; trenches at Grammar school and Boys' school dug.

White lines and Barriers: Painting lines on county and district roads, barriers at Boat float and Embankment. Notice boards cost £22 to erect.

Petrol pump: 300 gallons placed in tank adjacent to the Guildhall, pump hired on weekly basis. Petrol for emergency use only.

Bedding and blankets: Bedding, blankets, camp beds, towels, blinds, offices, helmets, etc. cost £130.

COMMANDOS IN DARTMOUTH November 1940 to May 1941

On 17th July, 1940 Admiral of the Fleet, Sir Roger Keyes, was made Director of Combined Operations stating that responsibilities included the raising, organising and training of special service troops later to be known as *Commandos*. Volunteers from all services were drafted in and training soon took place.

In November, 1940, soldiers of the No. 1 Special Service Battalion, commanded by Lt. Col. W. Glendinning, moved into the Dartmouth area for training along the coast, in the woods around the Dart and on Dartmoor. The headquarters was at Derwent Lodge and the quarter master's stores in the Warfleet Brewery.

A special subsistence allowance enabled troops to be billeted in Dartmouth for which landladies were paid 6s. 8d. per night, a large sum for those days. Accommodation was also at Kingswear, Dittisham and Stoke Fleming.

Training for special operations in enemy held land was intensive with soldiers on exercises night and day, amphibious landings along the nearby shoreline took place regularly, camping out around the Dart estuary, living off the land and engaging in mock attacks were frequently to be seen in the area.

Other activities took in early morning physical training, long distance marching often in full battle dress, weapon training with small arms, firing on ranges, small boat training, demolition practices and first aid procedures.

These soldiers during the winter of 1940-41 were well known to local people and it was upon this training that many of their later successful exploits were based.

However, their stay in Dartmouth was short lived. The large battalion was divided into Nos. 1 and 2 Commandos on 5th March, 1941, and in May, 1941, they were moved to Scotland where training areas were much more extensive.

On Training Exercises

Two photographs show commandos on a beach close to Dartmouth and surviving on Dartmoor where they had to live off the land. The plaque was presented to Dartmouth on the 50th anniversary of the formation of these troops on 5th March, 1991.

FOOD, CLOTHING AND FUEL RATIONING

Although it may not have been realised at the outbreak of the war that rationing at a local level would come in right away, the very heavy shipping losses sustained by the Allies when bringing in food and other supplies across the seas soon determined otherwise.

The Ministry of Food was, in fact, set up in 1937 and rationing right across the country started in the spring of 1940. Food was stored in very large depots and the country was divided into regions. People were allocated a ration book and clothing book and there was a Motor Fuel Ration Book for persons with authorised vehicle use.

One had to register with a grocer, butcher and milkman and remain with them unless the family moved away. Coupons were handed in for food and clothing in addition to money and this kept a very strict control on the amount people could buy. It must be said that supplies could sometimes be obtained on the black market and maybe bartering also took place.

However, the average housewife had to exercise great skill, sometimes patience and good judgement in using up the family coupons week by week. Various newspaper advertisements often offered advice in this matter; allowances change from time to time and rationing itself was not completely lifted until the early 1950s.

The weekly ration in May, 1941, was: 3 pints of milk, 9 ozs of jam, 7 ozs of butter, ½lb of sugar, 2 ozs of tea, 1/- worth of meat (rationed by price), 4 ozs of bacon, 1½ ozs of cheese and 2 ozs of cooking fat.

Clothes rationing came in on 1st June, 1941, and finished July, 1949. Coupons had to be handed in but people did not have to register with one shop. The allowance in 1941 was: shirt 5 coupons, main jacket 13 coupons, tie 1 coupon and so on. Each person had 66 coupons for a year, later reduced to 48, and utility clothes and furniture was introduced in 1942.

Once again housewives had to be very careful and often they resorted to making or modifying existing clothes or handing them down from one child to another.

THE NEW RATION BOOKS 1941

You will have to register again this time whether you wish to change your retailer or not. You can choose any retailer you like but it is best to register your whole family at the same shop. There is no need to go to the same shop for everything.

You must register between July 7 and 19. If you have not registered by July 19, you may not get your rations when your new Ration Books and your new registrations start on July 28.

HOW TO REGISTER

You will find counterfoils in both the Main Book, page 25 (page 23 in Child's Book) and in the Yellow Book (pages 12 and 13).

Fill in the counterfoils yourself. Do not ask the retailer to do it for you. He is very short of staff and has not the time.

MEAT, Yellow Book, page 13.
Fill in your name and address, your National Registration No., your Ration Book serial No., and the name and address of your butcher.

NOTE.—Write a large C on the Yellow Meat counterfoil which you fill in for your child if the child has a green Ration Book.

BUTTER, MARGARINE AND COOKING FATS,
Yellow Book, page 13.

On the butter and margarine counterfoil fill in your name and address, your National Registration No., your Ration Book serial No., and the name and address of your retailer.

NOTE.—Do not write on the counterfoil for cooking fats. You do not have to register separately for cooking fats but they must be bought from the same shop as your butter and margarine.

SUGAR AND PRESERVES,
Yellow Book, page 12.

Fill in your name and address, your National Registration No., your Ration Book serial No., and the name and address of your retailer.

NOTE.—Do not register for sugar and preserves separately. They must be bought from the same shop.

BACON AND HAM,
Yellow Book, page 13.
Fill in your name and address, your National Registration No., your Ration Book serial No., and the name and address of your retailer.

CHEESE, Main Book, page 25.
 Child's Book, page 23.
The counterfoil marked with a large B must be used. Fill in your name and address, your National Registration No., your Ration Book serial No., and the name and address of your retailer.

NOTE. — If you are entitled to the special 8 ozs. cheese ration do NOT use this counterfoil. Take your Ration Book to the Food Office between July 7 and 19.

EGGS.
If you have not yet registered for eggs do so at once using the counterfoil on the third spare page—page 14 of the old Ration Book. (Page 13, Child's Book.)

DO NOT CUT OUT ANY OF THE COUNTERFOILS. Take the book to the retailers concerned and they will cut them out.

Make sure you fill in the names and addresses of your NEW retailers inside the front and back covers of the Main Book, not your present retailers if you are changing.

Fill in the name and address of your present egg retailer in the blank space just below the bottom line on the inside of the back cover of the Main Book.

[Fill in *your own* name and address on the reference leaf— top section only (Main Book, page 3). Fill in the date of birth in the bottom section, if under 18. *Do not cut this page out.*]

THE MINISTRY OF FOOD, LONDON, S.W.1

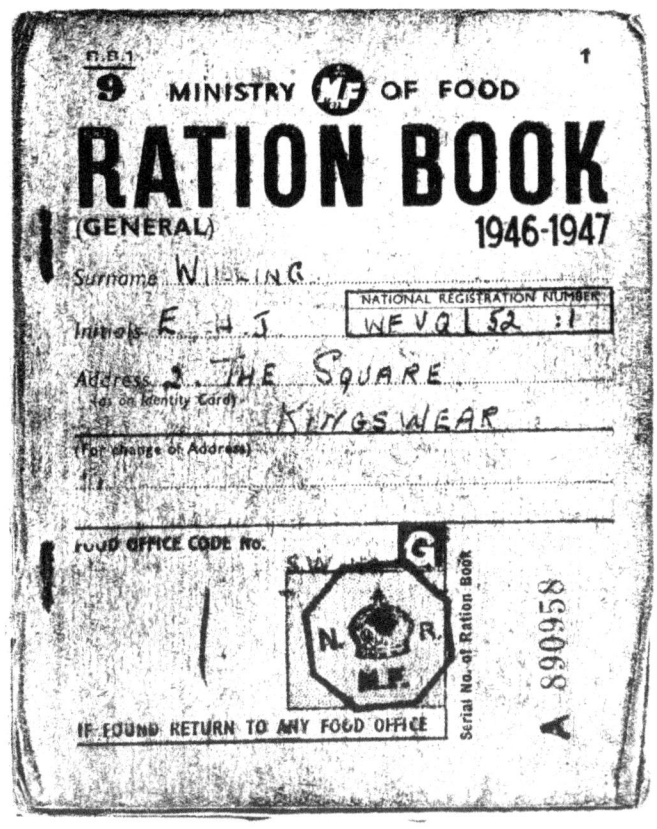

1942-43 CLOTHING BOOK

This book may not be used until the holder's name, full postal address and National Registration (Identity Card) Number have been plainly written below IN INK.

NAME *EDWIN H. J. WILLING*
(BLOCK LETTERS)

ADDRESS *"ALTA VISTA" CHURCH HILL*
(BLOCK LETTERS)

(TOWN) *KINGSWEAR* (COUNTY) *DEVON*

NATIONAL REGISTRATION (IDENTITY CARD) NUMBER
W.F.V.Q / 52 / 1.

Read the instructions within carefully, and take great care not to lose this book

HOW TO PUT ON YOUR GAS MASK

Always keep your gas mask with you – day and night. Learn to put it on quickly. Practise wearing it.

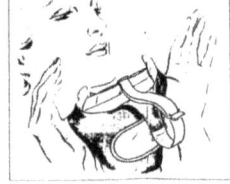 

1. Hold your breath. 2. Hold mask in front of face, with thumbs inside straps.
3. Thrust chin well forward into mask, pull straps over head as far as they will go.
4. Run finger round face-piece taking care head-straps are not twisted.

IF THE GAS RATTLES SOUND

1. Hold your breath. Put on mask wherever you are. Close window.
2. If out of doors, take off hat, put on your mask. Turn up collar.
3. Put on gloves or keep hands in pockets. Take cover in nearest building.

IF YOU GET GASSED

BY VAPOUR GAS Keep your gas mask on even if you feel discomfort. If discomfort continues go to First Aid Post

BY LIQUID or BLISTER GAS

1	2	3	4
Dab, but *don't rub* the splash with handkerchief. Then destroy handkerchief.	Rub No. 2 Ointment well into place. *(Buy a 6d. jar now from any chemist). In emergency chemists supply Bleach Cream free.*	If you can't get Ointment or Cream within 5 minutes wash place with soap and warm water	Take off at once any garment splashed with gas.

GAS MASK CASES

Morocco, 6/-

Morocco Finish, 3/6

Gas Masks

It was feared at the outbreak of the war that gas attacks would take place on civilians throughout the country. Gas masks were issued to all children and many adults and even babies could be kept in a gas hood covering them all over. It was a very common sight to see children carrying them to and from school; in May, 1941, a local article speaks of some not bothering to carry theirs but insisted they must. In August of the same year the masks were called in and fitted with more efficient filters free of charge and for many members of the Civil Defence they had to test out their masks by going into what was called a gas proof room this being in Smith's pharmacy shop (see Civil Defence section). However, by late 1941 the fear of an attack lessened and it was no longer compulsory to carry one although the majority of people kept theirs for the duration of the war. The poster was displayed throughout many towns advising of the handling of the mask.

Issue of Baby Gas Helmets

These details come from the Kingswear A.R.P. minute book:
Mary Saunders on 25.12.1941
Sally Peeke on 10.7.1939
Perdita Hutchinson on 4.4.1941
Pauline Monk on 21.4.1941
Peggy Lurse on 18.4.1942

Return of Baby Gas Helmets

Details from the same minute book read:
Mrs. Bellinger on 14.10.1941
Mrs. C. Hamlyn on 18.12.1941
Mrs. Evans on 7.1.1942
Vernice Miller on 29.4.1942
Mrs. Blackmore on 2.4.1942
Diane Westcott on 21.5.1942
Melvin Todd on 18.6.1942
Mary Saunders on 18.2.1943

No explanation was given for issuing or returning the masks.

Yacht Campeador V

This was Vernon MacAndrew's luxurious yacht which was blown up by a German mine near the Isle of Wight. Built at Philip's yard in 1938 he offered it to the Admiralty and it was commissioned on 18th September for use as a patrol boat along the Channel. It hit a mine on 22nd June, 1940, killing its owner and all but two of the twenty-two crew.

London Evacuees

Labelled and carrying gas masks children are seen here leaving their homes in London for various destinations throughout the country in 1940.

EVACUEES AT DARTMOUTH AND KINGSWEAR

The evacuation of children and adults from what was considered to be major target areas started on 1st September, 1939, three days before war was declared. By 3rd September nearly 1½ million people, mostly children, had been moved and by the end of the month 2 million had left their homes mainly from the London area.

As part of this national plan the whole of Acton Central School, London, came down by train arriving at Kingsbridge which was then the main reception centre for the South Hams. It was reported that there were 203 children with all the school staff under its headmaster Mr. S. Ewins. They left London at 10 a.m. and arrived at 4 p.m. tired, carrying a small rucsack and a gas mask. They were met by the billeting officer, given food and drink on the station and then allocated to different places throughout the area.

Eighty-one pupils, all boys except two girls so they could stay with their brothers, then came to Dartmouth on buses with Mr. Healey and Mr. Gwilt, teachers from Acton. They assembled at the Guildhall and local people were asked to take them in. It was the duty of the billeting officer to see that all were safely accommodated and to this end families were compelled to take in children when there were insufficient offers of help. Payment per week for the first child was 10/6d. (52½p), additional children was at the rate of 8/6d. (42½p).

The expected heavy bombing of London and other large cities did not occur so by the Spring of 1940 many of the evacuees returned to their homes. However, the situation changed dramatically when bombing started a few months later and this time about a 100 mothers with their children came to Kingswear by train, over to Dartmouth for allocation and once again new faces were seen in many requisitioned houses and local schools. This second large group also came from London this time from the East End. On this occasion boys from Victoria Road School were sent over to Kingswear to assist in the arrival.

So Dartmouth and Kingswear settled down to making the evacuees as comfortable and at home as much as possible. Friendships developed, some stayed on and married into Devon families, others joined the local defence units when of age and a few were caught up in the raids. As the war continued there were further evacuees but not in large groups.

Safely Arrived in Dartmouth

Doreen Tibbles and Connie Pitcher have settled in the home of Mr. and Mrs. De St. Pierre, Dartmouth, in early 1940 having left their homes in London. The Evacuation Scheme notice was often placed in windows showing that evacuees had been taken in and the occupants had accepted their allocation of children or adults.

CIVIL DEFENCE ORGANISATIONS

These were made up of the Special Constables, Air Raid Wardens, First Aid Parties, Red Cross, Fire Guards, Home Guards and the Womens' Voluntary Service. Warden posts and rest centres were also set up and the National and Auxiliary Fire Service had stations in the Market and at Central Hall Garage.

A large number of people served in these organisations; names often changed as members were called up for service and throughout the hostilities numerous exercises were held, usually at weekends, sometimes with the military forces.

The W.V.S. ran a restaurant on the South Embankment under Mrs. Harry assisted by about twenty helpers who provided a seven day service in preparing meals for the troops and, during the raids, tea and refreshments. This work continued throughout the war. Mr. W. T. Pillar played a prominent role in the A.R.P. which met in the Drill Hall. Equipped with a tin helmet, gas masks and whistle, wardens walked around the town during the raids while special constables ensured the blackout was maintained and order upheld. The photograph shows the A.R.P. rooms at Smith's pharmacy in Duke Street.

LOCAL DEFENCE VOLUNTEERS/HOME GUARD

On 14th May, 1940, the Secretary of State for War, the Rt. Hon. Anthony Eden, broadcast an appeal on the radio for volunteers to enlist in local defence units. This appeal was for men aged between 17 and 65 years and within a few days about 250,000 had responded by registering at their local police station or other reception points. So the Local Defence Volunteers were formed throughout the country. By July, 1940, there were over a million men registered for the defence of their localities.

On 28th July, 1940, Winston Churchill had the name changed to the Home Guard which remained until it was stood down in December, 1944. Almost every town had their local group of volunteer men kitted out with a uniform, armed with rifles and other small arms, regularly meeting for training, instruction and often called to duty when many towns were attacked by German planes.

Although for some months the equipment issued was improvised and not likely to prevent determined and highly trained enemy troops from occupying English soil, the men of the Home Guard had a very intimate knowledge of their own area which could have proved very valuable had an attack come.

The men of Dartmouth and Kingswear, young and not so young, volunteered at the Territorial Army Drill Hall, Clarence Hill, given arm bands with the letters "LDV" on them, divided into groups which were assigned to various assembly points. On the sounding of the siren the volunteers had to get to their positions as quickly as possible. Two of these were at the Castle and Gallant's Bower, others were around the town. The commander of the L.D.V. was Captain H. C. Lloyd, headmaster of the Grammar School who played a prominent role throughout the war later becoming Major in charge of the Warfleet Company of the Home Guard.

With the renaming of the L.D.V. uniforms, rifles, training sessions with lectures soon brought a level of efficiency and pride to the various Home Guard units on both sides of the estuary with many young men serving until they were called up into the services.

Training sessions took place at least once a week with weekend exercises from time to time and full scale exercises between troops in the area acting as the enemy, the Home Guard having to attack certain positions and label "the enemy" when caught.

The duties were numerous often at night when positions around the estuary had to be manned or guarded such as the guns at the Castle. Often the younger members of a unit acted as messengers either running or cycling when necessary. As the war went from year to year the Home Guard became more proficient in its organisation, equipment and undertaking of many duties. They sometimes operated with the services, engaged in supporting different arms of the services coming into the area and also provided social arrangements and games between platoons.

As Allied Forces moved into Europe the role of the Home Guard diminished in 1944. It was stood down in December of that year with parades and for the Warfleet Company a dinner in Dawe's Criterion Restaurant brought four years proud service to an end.

No. 2 Platoon, Longcross Company Home Guard, September 1942

Back row: A. Pepperel, Mr. Steer, E. Hull, D. Anderson, B. Anderson, platoon commander, Mr. Denley, T. Smith, F. Rutter, W. Tucker, L/Corporal Bennett and Corporal W. Huddy. *Front row:* A. Hayman, H. Goodman, Corporal Jones, T. Huddy and W. Hannaford.

Castle Battery Home Guard at Warfleet about 1943

Recognised are B. Holwill, J. Styles, R. Blake, D. Dunning, C. Callard, S. Waycott, L. Tucker, J. Rheberg, F. Hyne, S. Pound, Sgt. S. Rogers, L/Corporal J. Lidstone and F. Tooze. Nelson, the dog, acted as messenger. The men patrolled up Week Hill and the Ridges and met twice a week for lectures and practice.

EXTRACTS FROM A KINGSWEAR A.R.P. WARDEN'S MINUTE BOOK

It is fortunate that this book has survived which gives many details of meetings, events and people undertaking a wide variety of tasks during the years 1940 to 1942. It lists many people, social events for fund raising and even names and addresses of people serving in the forces. Some of the details are:

March, 1941: Members of the A.F.S. R. King, captain, R. Kelland, R. Hawke, E. Burrows, E. Marden, P. Little, L. Radford, A. Hunt and B. Pearn. Messengers Ken Dear and Reg. Thompson.

13th September, 1941: Electric clock fitted by Dartmouth Electric Works in A.R.P. office, Kingswear Hall.

30th October, 1941: Secondhand paraffin heater for post purchased for warden and post from Mr. S. Hall for 13/6. Spare wick in cupboard. Also ship's cabin lamp purchased for air raid shelter.

20th February, 1942: Blackout curtain is fitted in hall (long overdue).

February, 1942: Names of wardens. W. Fairweather, H. Williams, J. Fairweather, E. Martin, J. Wardsworth, J. Thompson, S. Northcott, J. Bissett, O. Oliver, W. Lueton, R. Sutton, P. Hopper, L. Heal, E. Towndrew, A. Roberts, J. Sharland, N. Rundle, Miss E. Williams (messenger), R. Little, J. Wallace and W. Wallace.

First Aid Party. R. Worth, C. Bray, C. Burrows, Mrs. M. Heal, Mrs. Clark and Robinson.

No. of fire guards in Kingswear: 150. Special constables: 22. Red Cross detachment: 15. A.R.P. personnel: 15. Rest centres' personnel: 8. Welfare committee: 20. Warden's post no. 83. First Aid post no. 83. Special Police H.Q., Kingswear Hall. A.R.P. H.Q. Fore Street (Lockup garage). Doctors: Dr. Hope Gill and Dr. Corbett.

June, 1942: Gas masks of the people living in Kingswear were examined by the wardens in Kingswear Hall on Tuesday, 9th June, Wednesday and Thursday.

17th March, 1941: A.R.P. room stocktaking: 13 steel helmets, 5 respirators, 7 suits anti-gas, 7 curtains anti-gas, 6 gloves pairs, 7 rubber boots, 10 eye shields, 1 stirrup pump, 3 rattles, 3 handbells, 5 whistles, 4 torches complete, 11 armlets blue, 1 warden post plate, 12 warden plates, 6 blankets, 1 map, 1 ointment anti-gas. The list was handed to Mr. H. B. Kauntze. Other items in store: 3 A.R.P. First Aid boxes. 8 warden bandages and 4 steel stretchers.

21st March, 1942: Alarm message received 15.40 Head Warden. During the next night alert a census of all persons using public shelters is to be taken by wardens. Returns must show the number of men, women and children (under fourteen) in three categories. If none, no return to be rendered. Message ends.

Kingswear A.F.S. Station, Fore Street

This 1940 photograph shows Peter Dudley, Ken Allen and one other fireman by the converted vehicle carrying a ladder and pulling a trailer pump close to the tank traps set in the road. The nissen-like building was erected on the roof of the lock-up garage where firemen slept and did their duty.

BRITANNIA ROYAL NAVAL COLLEGE

As this would have been a prime target for enemy troops landing in the area two steamers were requisitioned from Totnes, stored and provisioned, to take the Junior College up river should an attack come by land or by air.

From April, 1940, various steps were taken to defend the college buildings. The captain of the college took over as Naval Officer in charge of the port of Dartmouth, some of the lower passages in the building were made into shelters and after May, 1940, the senior College was organised into watches, fire parties, demolition and decontamination squads; staff enrolled in the Home Guard, the College clock bells were silenced and barbed wire was placed almost around the whole of the buildings.

A Special Service Company was also formed of volunteers limited to sixty and trained against paratroops in Mills bomb throwing, sten gun, revolver and rifle handling. The whole of the senior College was later brought into defend the College and house officers had live ammunition and grenades in their cabins in case of a night attack.

In 1940 a large contingent of W.R.N.S. arrived. Accommodation had to be found for them, an underground H.Q. and telephone exchange was set up under the terrace with an operations room and wireless transmitting room.

Other changes included building gunnery and torpedo huts for training, the band practice room became the aircraft recognition centre and even the beagles were disbanded and their kennels used for housing pigs!

The College defence units were involved in full scale exercises in the Dartmouth area one taking place in the very cold winter of 1942 when water froze in some of the cadet's water bottles and two of the Home Guard died.

On 18th September, 1942, Dartmouth was attacked in a daylight raid causing serious damage to Noss Works, some boats on the river and two bombs falling on the College, one on B block and the other on the quarter deck. Fortunately the cadets were still on vacation but one W.R.N.S. personnel was killed. The photograph below shows part of the damage.

The College staff and cadets were moved for safety in early 1943 first to Bristol and then for the rest of the war years at Eaton Hall, Cheshire, staying there until 1946.

Soon after the evacuation of the College U.S. troops made it their local H.Q. transforming much of the interior of the building and occupying it until after the Normandy Landings of 6th June, 1944. Then it was used by other forces finally reverting to having its own cadets in 1946.

Bomb Damage to the College

The New headmaster, J.W. Stork, had just arrived at the start of a new term when this disaster occurred. At the time of the impact of the two bombs a meeting was in progress in the Commando's cabin planning the evacuation of the college should it be attacked. No one was hurt, lights went out and all the windows on the south side of D block were blown out with wall and roof damage occurring as partly seen in this photograph.

FREE FRENCH FORCES

There was a French presence here for most of the war. The fall of Dunkirk resulted in hundreds of French vessels making for the safety of the English coast among which were two tugs, *L'Isère* and *L'Aube*, that came to the Dart where they were taken over to do duty up and down the estuary. There were also many French sailors here; later in 1941 a French destroyer, manned by R.N. personnel, came into the harbour almost hitting rocks while turning and a report of the same year stated that five deaths occurred on a French submarine *Chaser* while in the harbour.

However, the Free French Forces took on a definite role when the 2nd Division of the 20th M.L. Flotilla was formed with their base at Portsmouth. The division was stationed at Kingswear and was made up of four vessels. They were mainly engaged in coastal escort duties, defensive patrols and air sea rescue work until 1942. In August of that year they were restructured as part of the newly formed 23rd Flotilla equipped with eight new motor torpedo boats crewed by French personnel with three English liaison officers. It was this unit which undertook patrols from Kingswear for the rest of the war and were among the first French vessels to enter Brest harbour in 1945.

The advance party of the 23rd Flotilla came in January, 1943; H.Q. was at Brookhill where ratings were also billeted while officers were at Longford. Overall command came under English coastal forces whose H.Q. was H.M.S. *Cicala*, the Royal Dart Hotel. The unit was made up of a depot ship, eight M.T.Bs. and it carried out 451 patrols including 128 enemy engagements sinking five German ships. The M.T.Bs. suffered damage from time to time, crews were injured but there were no losses but many close encounters.

Most of the engagements took place off the French coast under cover of darkness. The boats would normally leave Kingswear during the early evening making good speed for the enemy shipping lanes. They were powered by three Packard engines and two Ford auxiliary engines capable of 40 knots with a range of 420 miles and manned by 14 crew. Armament was two torpedos, various guns, depth charges, hand grenades and smoke screen apparatus.

In August, 1944, the flotilla was transferred to Brittany where the French crews were at last serving on their own ground. The boats returned to Kingswear on 25th September, 1944, and took their leave two days later after a farewell evening at Kingswear so bringing to an end a long and very successful association with this area.

Loading Torpedos at Kingswear

M.T.B. 96 is being armed with two 21" torpedos at the jetty at Kingswear sometime in 1943. There was a French depot ship here *Belfort*; the torpedos were stored in nearby nissen huts and fuel was in four large tanks sited just below Hoodown House and gravity fed down to the boats.

Wartime Reports for 1940

Evacuees New Year's Party

About 120 evacuated children sat down to tea in the Guildhall with the Mayoress, Mrs. W.G. Row. 50 were from Acton Central School, the remainder being voluntary evacuees. Entertainment was organised by Mrs. Vera Tolman, games by Mr. Leslie Thorne and Mr. L.B. Thorne. Mr. J.E. Gardner, Dartmouth Area Officer, said the party was a great success. *January 1940*

Fire Brigade for Kingswear

A crew of eight is to be formed. Kingswear is to have its own fire brigade said Mr. W.L. Fairweather. One trailer would be allocated requiring eight volunteers with four others as a reserve. Mr. G.E. Turner said that 25 men were already engaged in the A.R.P. and 22 as special constables. *May 1940*

Dartmouth Blackout Warning

Future offenders to be taken to court. A final warning to Dartmouth blackout offenders was issued by the Mayor, Alderman W.G. Row, at the Police Court on Tuesday.

The blackout now commences at 9.30p.m. and everyone should be in bed by midnight. The police and regular reserves are tired of going around warning people of lights being seen. *May 1940*

Gas Masks to be Carried

Police reminder to Dartmouth. Superintendent Barncott reminded the public of Dartmouth and District that everyone is expected to carry his or her own gas mask. Anyone who appears in the street not carrying one will be stopped by the police. *May 1940*

Public Shelters in Dartmouth

£300 to be spent on six sites. Provision of permanent public shelters is planned for at Market Square, Collaford Lane, Manor Gardens, The Pound, Ford Cross and at Victoria Road. Plans by the borough engineer will be submitted to the county for approval. An appeal was also made for first aid members. Mr. Lee-Wright of the Boat House, South Town, who also had volunteered the use of his car and trailer for this work was praised. *7 June 1940*

Police ask You to carry your Gas Masks
Gas Mask cases at 2/6
and in Morroco 6/- at Cranfords

German Gun to Go

Dartmouth Town Council has agreed to hand over the old German gun on the Putting Green, South Embankment, to the Salvage Depot of the Ministry of Supply as part of the campaign for the collection of scrap metal.

The Mayor stated yesterday that the council did not contemplate disposing of any other scrap metal which may be in its possession in a similar way up to the present. *June, 1940*

Black Out Signs

Shop signs and names on vans and lorries conveying information as to the identity of Dartmouth are being removed or painted over by Darmouth shopkeepers this week following the order issued by the Government.

There are still several, however, that have not been obliterated and Sgt. J. Perryman has reminded business people that this is now compulsory. *June 1940*

New Ration Book Reminder

Risk being left without coupons. Mr. J.C. Gardner, Dartmouth food executive officer, said that there are still many local housewifes who have not yet applied for the new ration books for the next period starting 8th July 1940. *June 1940*

Bombs in Fields

Raiders flight from fighters. Two bombs were dropped on farmland in a neighbouring district doing no damage or injury. The planes passed over Dartmouth at great speed and smoke could be seen rising in the distance. *July 1940*

Fight for Girl in Dance Hall

Police Sgt. Perryman said a dance was in progress in a hall in Flavel Street attended by English, French and Belgian sailors with other aliens. A French seaman was summoned for being drunk and disorderly in Flavel Street and he pleaded guilty.

A Danish seaman was also summoned for being drunk and disorderly on the South Embankment and was fined 5s. with 10d. costs. *July 1940*

The Spitfire Fund

Thermometer to show how total is growing. The Dartmouth, Kingswear and District Spitfire Fund which was started last week has reached £243. The proceeds of the Dartmouth Cricket Club's whist in the Central Hall realised £1.11s.6d. Collections boxes will be placed in the town and thermometer will be fixed in Mr. C.H. Dawe's Criterion restaurant window on The Quay. *July 1940*

300 at Ball - Spitfire Fund

A company of 300 people attended a ball in the Guildhall on August Bank Holiday in aid of the Dartmouth, Kingswear and District Spitfire Fund. Music was by Henry Pearce and his band, from Torquay. Arrangements were by Mr. and Mrs. J.A. Phillip, Mr. and Mrs. B.C. Kirk, Mr. and Mrs. J.C. Stoneman, Mr. and Mrs. W.J. Horrell, Mr. and Mrs. F.C. Holwill and Mr. and Mrs. F.M. Tolman. The whole of the profits of the bar will also go to the Spitfire Fund. *August 1940*

Six whole time Fireman Wanted

The Fire Brigade Committee considered the question of relief for the two drivers of cars used for towing trailer pumps. Chief Officer J. Lyons reported that in addition to Mr. C. Young and Mr. R.C. Pillar, Mr. F. Mitchelmore and Mr. W.E. Lord had offered assistance. Mr. C. Young had offered to loan his caravan to be placed in Market Square for sleeping purposes.

The strength of the Fire Brigade was 3 officers, 12 firemen, 1 turncock and the auxiliary fire brigade 21 firemen, 8 messengers and 3 telephonists. *August 1940*

AIR RAID SHELTERS

Many people will recall these shelters as they often slept in them or used them during air raids and those built above ground were a familiar sight to local people for most of the war years. Dartmouth had a variety of private and public shelters; those for the house being *Morrison* shelters, those for the garden *Anderson* shelters while many people built their own from lengths of timber covered with sand bags.

Public shelters were normally above ground built with brick and reinforced concrete to hold dozens if not hundreds of people. The size of the shelter was often determined by its location and the number of people living nearby. Dartmouth had a variety of these located in different parts of the town and their construction started in March, 1940, continuing into 1942. They were, in fact, planned nationally in 1938 when it was realised that England would be open to attack by high explosive bombs.

Five were planned for Dartmouth in late 1939 these being at Old Vaults in Coronation Park; Hawke's Store in Mayor's Avenue; Adam's Store in Lower Street; Denning's Store and Old Rieve's Store at Bayard's Cove. Later a large one was built close to the Boat Yard. They could hold 540 people and cost £103.18s. to build.

Others were later built in the playground of Victoria Road Boys' School and one was built for the senior boys in the quarry above the school. Another was in the Noss Works, two at Kingswear and down by the gun site close to the castle. No doubt readers will recall others in the area as in the October, 1940, newspaper report.

Various complaints were recorded in the local press often referring to the lack of sanitation, poor seating or inadequate lighting often just with hurricane lamps.

However, many did prove their worth during the raids on the town while others provided a safe refuge during air raid warnings.

Anderson Shelter

Named after Sir John Anderson, they were planned in December 1938 and were supplied free of charge to some two and a half million families in the main target areas. They comprised of steel corrugated sheeting lowered into a 4 ft. pit normally dug in a garden then covered over with earth and turf. They gave good protection for six people but were often damp and flooded in times of heavy rain.

Morrison Shelter

Named after Herbert Morrison, Minister of Home Security, a steel top and heavy wire framed sides provided good protection for a family and it proved to be useful as a table as well. Half a million were distributed by the end of 1941 the majority being free. People often slept in them as a matter of course.

Old Gas Masks Incomplete
Another reminder to householders. A reminder of the necessity for all gas masks to be fitted with the new contex fitter extension was made yesterday by Mr. J.C. Gardner, A.R.P. officer in charge. Wardens are on duty day and night at the Drill Hall, Clarence Hill, where the job of fitting the filter will only take a few minutes. *30 August 1940*

First Black Out Charge
The first case of a black out offence was heard at Dartmouth's Police Court on Tuesday when Miss Bessie D. Ross of Clarence Hill was fined 5s. for having an unscreened window at her house at 11.15 p.m. on 27th August 1940. *13 September 1940*

Old Tunnels as Shelters
Sites for four more public air raid shelters in Dartmouth have been agreed upon by the local Civil Defence Committee. They are at Royal Avenue Gardens in front of the bandstand. Anzac Square where the old jail's two cells are to be cleaned and electricity to be installed. Mount Boone tunnel under the roadway is to be adapted by the local people at their own cost of £14.00. Little work was needed only a lock and key and a few hurricane lamps were required. *October 1940*

Cottage Wrecked by Bomb
Wife rescued from ruin by husband. One of four bombs dropped by a solitary German plane in a district in the south west wrecked two cottages and buried Mrs. Fred Jane, wife of the occupant, under the debris. The bomb made a crater in the lane and reduced the cottages to rubble. Mr. John Coaker, from a nearby farm, helped in the rescue; three other bombs fell harmlessly on farmland. *November 1940*

Wartime Reports for 1941

New Siren at Dartmouth
More than £40 will be spent on installing a new siren at the Market Hall. A new 4 h.p. Gent siren will be installed by Messrs. H. Anderson and Sons at a cost of £28.10s. The bill for wiring by the Urban Electric Supply Company Ltd. totals £12.10s. *January 1941*

Missing Sailor Safe
Mr. J. Hearn, a P.O.W. in Germany. After being mourned as dead for seven months Mr. Jack Hearn of Above Town Dartmouth, has returned, as it were, from the dead. On Monday his sister Mrs. V. McLeod received a letter from him saying he was a prisoner in Germany but was okay. Aged 26 he was born in Dartmouth and joined the mercantile marine at the outbreak of war. *March 1941*

Day Nursery at Warfleet
Another addition to Dartmouth's homes for evacuees is a nursery centre at Warfleet House to be opened shortly under the supervision of Miss H.L. Pickett. *March 1941*

New Head Warden
Mr. B.E. Hanson was appointed head warden of the borough succeeding Mr. W.J. MacDonald who had done good work as a warden. *April 1941*

War Weapon's Week 24-31 May 1941
Dartmouth's target is £35,000. Mr. Dawe has kindly placed his shop on the Quay at the disposal of Dartmouth's War Weapons Week Committee as a selling centre. *May 1941*

Incendiary Bomb Demonstrations
These will be held at the following places and the public are invited to attend. Junction of Higher Street and Newcomen Road, Manor House, Union Square, Ford Cross, Market Square, Avenue Gardens, Coronation Park, St. George's Square, Mount Boone House and at the Island, Britannia Avenue. Guildhall, Dartmouth, 29th May 1941. J.C. Gardner, Town Clerk.

Plymouth Evacuees
Arrangements were made last month to receive in Dartmouth 50 unaccompanied children from Plymouth with a further 50 more that the Lord Mayor of Plymouth would like to send. *June 1941*

Shopkeepers for the R.A.F.
Call up for the forces and industry. Several Dartmouth traders have been affected by recruiting. They are Mr. R.J. Sanders, baker and confectioner, under the business name of E.A. Wallis, Foss St., Mr. Rudd Prynn, proprietor of Rudd Prynn and Comp. outfitters, Duke St., who is going into the R.A.F., Mr. L.G. Hodge, fruiterer at 2 Newcomen Road, Mr. A.J. Bates, 31 Townstal Road, plumbing business and Mr. A.W. Tozer printer with the *Dartmouth Chronicle* who at 31 leaves on Wednesday for the R.A.F. *July 1941*

Acton School Boys leave Dartmouth
Another batch is expected next month but 14 have returned to Acton Central School having spent two years in Dartmouth. All will have reached the age of 16 years by the end of this term. During their stay 10 of them belonged to the A.T. Corps and they will transfer to the Acton A.T. Corps. *July 1941*

Air Raid Shelters at Kingswear
More shelters are requested to accommodate 50 or more people to ensure their safety. A suitable site would be near the slipway adjoining the present brick shelter. There is also a shelter higher up at the main road which is in need of repair. *August 1941*

Air Raid Rehearsal
Miss McGrath, matron of Dartmouth hospital, organised a full scale blitz practice for the hospital and ambulance services last Thursday. The hospital annexe was used coping with a never ending stream of "casualties", school boys and girls, soldiers and sailors each person being given a label saying what they should do. *September 1941*

Dartmouth to lose its Iron Gates and Railings
The town council decided to object to the Ministry of Supply's request for the scraping of the two guns in the area, one being a Russian. Railings, gates, posts, chains, bollards and similar articles in the district will be removed under the direction of a new Railings Officer. 25s. will be paid for each ton of scrap collected for those asking for compensation. *October 1941*

Dartmouth Men together in a German Camp
The first letter giving names of the Dartmouth men who disappeared with the Royal Marines in the Battle of Crete came from Mr. Cecil Perring of 4 Charles Street. He is in good health and is with other Dartmouth men, Mr. Jack Lear, Mr. Fred McCall and Mr. Leslie Saunders. *November 1941*

Cadets for R.A.F.
First two postings from Dartmouth's A.T.Corps. B. Pearn of Kingswear who has been in the A.T.Corps since last May has been awarded the A.T.C. cup for high marks and will start his training as a pilot officer and cadet D. Green has gone to be trained as a gunner. *December 1941*

Dartmouth's Food Office
Free distribution is being made from this office of cod liver oil, blackcurrent juice, fruit juice and black currant puree to children under two years of age. *December 1941*

Scrap Collected in October 1941
During this month Dartmouth collected and sold two tons of waste paper, two tons of cardboard, 17½ tons of scrap metal and six cwts. of bones valued at £46.14s. Salvage receipts from 1st April, 1941, now total £134.10s.10d. *December 1941*

Wartime Reports for 1942
Comforts for Russia
In the three months ending 31st December, 1941, Kingswear Red Cross Working party sent 677 garments, comforts and hospital bandages etc. to the regional office in Devon, the Red Cross depot in Torquay and to local members of the services. Included were helmets and sea-boot stockings for Russia.

Gifts also include felt for slipper soles from Mrs. Hine-Haycock, and knitted comforts from Mrs. Evelyn, Miss Pearl and Mrs. Witton. The Committee comprises of Mrs. West, Secretary and treasurer. Mrs. Melville, Mrs. Turner and Miss Blackborow. *January 1942*

Dartmouth Flight
Now a separate unit of the Air Training Corps

The Dartmouth Flight which previously formed part of the Paignton A.T.C. has been given independent status. It was administered under Instructor Commander Baldwin, R.N., Instructor Commander Sobey, R.N., treasurer Mr. W.T. Harris, M.A., and Councillor E.A.W. Gray, F/Officer J.C. Stoneman is o/c with P/Officer R.W. Morris as second officer. The flight has been affiliated to an aerodrome for periodic visits. Five cadets will spend two days away and in March, 1942, twenty four are due to go for visiting and some training. *February 1942*

Home Guard Recruits
A large number of boys, aged 15 to 18, have joined Dartmouth's Home Guard as a result of an appeal by Lt. Col. D.G. Robinson, its commanding officer. *March 1942*

Air Training Corps - 1877 Flight Dartmouth Flight Orders
For week ending 13 June 1942

Monday 8 June:	19.00 hrs.	Parade at R.NC. gate
Tuesday 9 June:	18.00 hrs.	Parade at Sandquay, shooting instruction.
Thursday 11 June:	11.00 hrs.	March to R.N.C.
	19.30 hrs.	Mathematics, 3 classes.
	20.00 hrs.	Navigation.
	21.00 hrs.	Dismiss parade.
Friday 12 June:	18.45 hrs.	College gates flight drill.
	19.30 hrs.	Armaments.
	20.00 hrs.	Aircraft recognition.
Saturday 13 June:		Cricket.

F/Officer J.C. Stoneman, R.A.F.V.R.

Morris Shelters in Demand
Large families to be supplied first. Dartmouth has been allotted 750 indoor Morrison shelters. A consignment has already arrived and discussions are to take place as to who will have free shelters and who will have to pay £7 for each. *July 1942*

Awards to Special Constables
The chief constable of Devon made awards to Dartmouth's special constables these being Area Officer W.S. Bindlos, assistant area officer A.E. Singer, Sgt. F.M. Tolman, Sgt. S.R. Sanders, special constables C.F. Akhirst, J.B. Cottle, H.B. Couch, W.H. Favis, W.F. Smith, J.P. Tolman. Medals were also given to G.A. Atkins, R.F. Couzens, R. Foyle, W.A. Gill, F.C. Holwill, W.J. Horrell, G.V. Penistone and F.J. Robertson. *August 1942*

Kingswear A.R.P. Social
This was held in the Kingswear Hall on Monday with members of the A.R.P. and friends. Lt. Cook, gave an hour's concert; a short sketch on the works of the A.R.P. was given by Lt. Carsen and Lt. Cook. Commander Yardley, Captain and T. Witton, Mr. Hugh Goodson and Mr. H.B. Kauntze (head warden rural area) were amongst those present.

Refreshments were served by Mr. and Mrs. Stanleick, songs by Mr. Dart, Mr. A.E. Martin, Mr. J. Thompson, Mr. W.L. Fairweather and Mr. R.J. Worth. Mr. H.G. Williams, Group Warden at Kingswear, is leaving to take up duties elsewhere. *December 1942*

DARTMOUTH & KINGSWEAR WARSHIP WEEK

March 14th—21st 1942

Programme of Events

SATURDAY, MARCH 14th.

11. 0 a.m.—Opening of Indicator—Dawe's Cafe.
3.15 p.m.—Parade and Procession—Coronation Park.
   LORD LOUIS MOUNTBATTEN, G.C.V.O., D.S.O., R.N., will take the salute.
4. 0 p.m.—The Band of the Anti-Tank Regt., R.A., will BEAT THE RETREAT opposite the Guildhall.
4.30 p.m.—INAUGURAL CEREMONY in the Guildhall.
   Speakers: Lord Louis Mountbatten, G.C.V.O., D.S.O., R.N.; C. Williams, M.P.
   Chairman: His Worship the Mayor (Alderman W. G. Row).
7.30 p.m.—TOPICAL NAUTICAL REVUE, "AFLOAT and ASHORE," Guildhall, Dartmouth.
   Admission 2/6, 1/6. Seats reserved at Messrs. Cranfords, Fairfax Place.

SUNDAY, MARCH 15th.

3. 0 p.m.—CIVIC SERVICE at St. Saviour's Church.
   The Mayor and Corporation and Local Organisations will march from the Guildhall, 2.45 p.m. Royal Marine Band.
8. 0 p.m.—BAND and VOCAL CONCERT, Guildhall, Dartmouth. Band of the Royal Marines.
   Kathleen Palmer, George Dalton, Leonard Durrant, William J. Harris.
   All seats 1/- at the Door.

MONDAY, MARCH 16th.

DANCE Guildhall, Dartmouth.
WHIST TOURNAMENT, Kingswear Hall.

TUESDAY, MARCH 17th.

3. 0 p.m.—WHIST DRIVE, Foresters' Hall, Dartmouth.
7.30 p.m.—DANCE, Guildhall, Dartmouth.
7.30 p.m.—DANCE, Kingswear Hall, Kingswear.

WEDNESDAY, MARCH 18th.

3. 0 p.m.—PLAY, "The QUEEN'S HUSBAND," at the Royal Naval College. Admission 3/-, 2/-, 1/-. All bookable at Messrs. Cranfords, Fairfax Place. Phone 24.
7.30 p.m.—BOXING TOURNAMENT, Guildhall, Dartmouth. REGULARS v LOCAL SERVICES.
   TED (KID) LEWIS will be in attendance.
   Admission 5/-, 3/6. Seats reserved at "Wise," Tobacconists, The Quay, Dartmouth. 2/6, 1/3 Unreserved.
7.30 p.m.—GRAND VARIETY CONCERT, Kingswear Hall, Kingswear. Admission 2/-, 1/-.

THURSDAY, MARCH 19th.

7.30 p.m.—DANCE, Guildhall, Dartmouth. Admission 2/6, 1/6.
7.30 p.m.—DANCE and CABARET, Kingswear Hall, Kingswear. Valeries' Vanities from Queen's Hotel, Torquay. Band — Clemsons Debonnaires. Ticket 5/-

FUND RAISING IN THE WAR

The people of Dartmouth and Kingswear, like many other communities, responded with great enthusiasm when called upon to raise funds to support various armament programmes or aid to prisoners, the Red Cross, Russian Flag Day, etc.

Targets were set and often exceeded during savings weeks which could be easily seen by the local people in the form of a large "thermometer" showing the monies coming in. All kinds of events were organised, the Home Guard laying on demonstrations, concerts arranged, etc. as shown on this page when the programme for the Warship Week was drawn up for March, 1942.

The first call on the people of Dartmouth and Kingswear was the Spitfire Fund in January, 1941, for which nearly £2,000 was raised by the end of February. Then came an appeal for £35,000 for a warship during April, 1941, followed by War Weapons Week in May when £25,000 was raised on the first day and a total of £137,021 collected for the week.

In March, 1942, another Warship Week was launched, the programme of which is on this page and in December, 1942, £200 was raised for the Prisoners' Fund to send food parcels, etc. to men imprisoned in Germany.

£18,000 was the target in February, 1943, for a fighter plane which was exceeded. June heralded Wings for Victory Week when sufficient funds came in for eighteen fighter planes; £200 was raised for the Prisoners' Fund in September, £672 raised for Sailor Week in October the year closing with Merchant Week in November realising £1,357 and an Aid for Russian Flag Day also took place.

Earl Mount Batten opened Salute the Soldier Week in May, 1944; by June the target had been easily passed and an Aid for China Week followed closely. In October £672 was raised for Sailor Week and £12,728 for the Red Cross in December.

Apart from these reported events there was the National Savings Movement and no doubt many other means of saving or contributing to the war effort. Such a record during these years when there were all kinds of shortages is one to be very proud of and shows quite clearly the commitment of the local people living on either side of the Dart.

FRIDAY, MARCH 20th.

WOMEN'S SOCIAL MEETING, Guildhall, Dartmouth. 3. 0 p.m.
Speakers: Miss Knight Bruce, Mrs. B. Cunlifé.
Entertainment. Refreshments. Admission Free.
GRAND VARIETY CONCERT, Guildhall, Dartmouth. Admission 2/-, 1/-. Bookable at Messrs. E. Hawke Ltd., Duke Street, Dartmouth. 7.30 p.m.

SATURDAY, MARCH 21st.

CORONATION PARK. Demonstrations by Mobile Instructional Bus and Lewis Gun Display, also Display and Beating of the Retreat by the Boys of the Brixham Naval Orphanage. 3.15 p.m.
GRAND BALL, Guildhall, Dartmouth. 8. 0 p.m. Admission 6/-.
PUBLIC ANNOUNCEMENT of Financial Result by His Worship The Mayor from Balcony of Guildhall, Dartmouth. 9. 0 p.m.

RAID ON PHILIP AND SON, SHIPBUILDERS AND ENGINEERS, 18th SEPTEMBER, 1942

This company made a major contribution to the war effort by constructing 230 vessels at the Sandquay and Noss Works employing almost 600 people for the duration of the hostilities.

Vessels were built for the Admiralty and the R.A.F. among which were corvettes, minesweepers, minelayers, air sea rescue launches, refuelling launches, naval armament vessels for carrying large guns, tugs and boom defence vessels. Two vessels are shown here, the upper is a boom defence vessel, H.M.S. *Barflake* and the lower is an R.A.F. Air Sea Rescue launch, No. 1319.

It was reported in the local press that six M.E. 109s flew down the Dart estuary then pairing off to attack Noss Works, vessels on the river and the Naval College. One bomb fell on the company penetrating the mould loft and then exploding by hitting a girder in the plating loft. The very extensive damage can be seen in the photographs over page. This was the most serious raid of the war in terms of casualties. Flying shrapnel and equipment killed twenty people injuring a further 40 many being taken to Torbay hospitals. There was an immediate response from units of Kingswear and Dartmouth Civil Defence Corps; doctors, nurses and ambulances were quickly on the scene rendering every possible aid.

In spite of extensive damage the yard was partly working after about forty-eight hours then managed by Mr. R. Stewart.

```
Dartmouth.         At approx. 1130/18 the following damage was caused
                   to R.N.College Dartmouth.
                   (S.C.E.Devonport 2000/18.)
      Casualties. Philips Noss Works machine shop wrecked.  Coal
hulk DAGNY sunk.      Collier FERNWOOD sunk.  Pontoon crane
with grab for coaling sunk.M.L.155 leaking badly.    H.M.S.SELKIRK
minor damage and leaks.  R.F.A. BERTA reports diesel and fuel oil
contaminating each other and water contaminating both.
(Lt.Brammal 2000A/18, N.O.I.C.Dartmouth 2225/18.)
```

Damaged Workshops
Only the heaviest of the engineering equipment withstood the blast as shown above. The large cutting and punching machine stands amidst the ruins while to the right the galvanised roof was stripped leaving the framework uncovered.

Looking North
This view is up river and shows some of the debris put to one side clearing an access road to the main area of the damage on the left. Even here one side frame of a workshop stands forlorn.

Top of the Building Berths

Another view of the damage showing the work's chimney stack to the left and a crane put out of action. Corrugated roofing lies in the foreground.

Havoc Abounds

Three men are viewing the ruins by the yard's rail track. The forecastle of a corvette is in the background; the scene close to the plating shop clearly shows the extent of the blast damage.

The Mud Berth

In the foreground is a yacht in for the winter; the cutting machine stands exposed in the background to the right with an end section of a building dangerously standing without support.

Wartime Reports for 1943
Enemy Raider Destroyed
A Fock Wolfe plane was brought down with a direct hit as it crossed the coast at Slapton Sands bursting into flames when it hit the ground crashing through two hedges. The pilot was killed. *March 1943*

Home Guard's 3rd Birthday
Part of the celebrations took the form of shooting at a dummy tank by members of the Warfleet Company. The tank was set up at Jawbones and 18 rounds of ammunition were accurately fired at the tank setting it alight. The demonstration was conducted by MacCormac. *May 1943*

Victory Cheers
Townspeople received the news of the unconditional surrender of Italy on Wednesday night with great jubilation. During a dance at Dartmouth's Guildhall, Mr. F.C. Sanders, M.C., stopped the music and gathered the happy throng before him and asked them to remember the men who had made this victory possible. He led three cheers for the victory armies and the national anthem was sung. Groups gathered in the streets to discuss the announcement made on the 6 p.m. B.B.C. news. *September 1943*

Mr. D.L. Gibson, Radio Engineer
Wishes to inform his customers that he has now been called to His Majesty's Service. Business will be carried on at 19 Newcomen Road and every care and attention will be given to orders. *October 1943*

Gas Exercise
Townspeople were wakened recently on a Sunday morning by the sounding of a gas alarm. W.T. Pillar, A.R.P. Officer, was at the incident staged on the Quay where real gas was used and the decontamination squad was called in. Police constables and members of the Dartmouth Army Cadet Force co-operated. *November 1943*

80,000 Meals in a Year
Force's club spendid service. Dartmouth Market Square Force's Club provided 80,000 meals during the past year. This was reported at its first annual meeting. Mr. L.J. Annereau, secretary, and Mr. J.R. Peebe, treasurer. Sales had realised £1,010. *November 1943*

Fire Guard at Dartmouth
The regional exercise arranged for Thursday 30th December, 1943, will start at 7.30 p.m. and close about one hour later. An alert will sound at 7.30 p.m. and fire guards will stand in their street party in readiness for action. Steel helmets and armlets will be worn. F.E. Spencer, Fire Guard Officer, Headquarters 14 The Quay. *November 1943*

Wartime Reports for 1944
A Combined Exercise
This will be held on Saturday, 15th January, 1944, at 14.00 hours. The public are warned to have their respirators examined and to carry same as gas will be used. Samuel Harvey, sub-controller. *January 1944*

Smoke blanket envelopes South Town
A great smoke blanket enveloped part of South Town on Monday evening and caused considerable discomfort to householders and people in the vicinity. Several were completely overcome and received medical attention. This was the unhappy outcome of a demonstration staged by Dartmouth's Fire Guard Dept. in co-operation with the N.F.S. under Mr. G. Speare, regional officer.

It was designed to show how to tackle phosphorous bombs and to show how wardens could assist the Fire Guards and N.F.S. Smoke generators were used placed at Manor House by Mr. W. Archer-May who released their contents. The smoke was thicker than intended, clouds of gas causing many streaming eyes, acute coughing among those taking part including Mr. May who shortly recovered. *June 1944*

Ration Book Issue
It was announced at the last meeting of Dartmouth's Food Control Committee that the issue of the new ration books was almost complete and thanks were extended to Miss Blarney, Mr. and Mrs. Russell and Miss Frewin for the help they had volunteered. *June 1940*

Kingswear Receives Evacuees
Three groups of mothers and children evacuees from London arrived during the last fortnight making 50 in total. The reception arrangements had been made by Miss Oliver in Kingswear Hall. More evacuees are expected. *July 1944*

Borough of Dartmouth, National Emergency
Owing to the limited water supply the following restrictions will apply. Water will be turned off from 6 p.m. to 6 a.m. each day until further notice. Washing of cars, pavements and watering of gardens is strictly prohibited until further notice. *August 1944*

100% Blackout to be Maintained
A warning that it is still necessary to maintain a complete blackout was issued at Dartmouth Police Court when Walter Collard, 16 Clarence Place, was fined 5s. for an offence against the regulations. *August 1944*

Airman Decorated
First award to a former Dartmouth A.T.C. cadet Ft/Lt. H.H. Hancock has been awarded the D.F.C. for meritorious service. He learnt of the award last week while on leave at his home. *December 1944*

General's son a Prisoner
News has reached Brigadier General and Mrs. H. LLewylln of Nethway House, Kingswear, that their son, Lt. A.D. Llewylln of the Scots Guards who was reported wounded and missing some weeks ago is a prisoner in Germany. *December 1944*

Rescues from Debris after Many Hours

WOMEN AND CHILDREN GUNNED IN THE STREETS

RAID ON DARTMOUTH: 13th FEBRUARY, 1943

This was the most serious raid on the town itself occurring at about 11.30 a.m. on Saturday, 13th February, when two enemy planes came in low from the sea dropping two high explosive bombs killing fifteen people and injuring about forty. The first bomb fell on the public house *Town Arms* and the adjacent grocery shop in Higher Street; the second fell on buildings standing along Duke Street and Foss Street destroying five and extensively damaging others around them. The photographs give a good idea of the damage. Damage was also caused to the Girls' council school in Higher Street and straffing by machine gun fire caused some of the casualties and damage to property away from the site of the two bombs. A full list of those who died is listed from the War Grave Commission documents.

There were no casualties in the *Town Arms* public house in spite of many customers drinking but Mr. and Mrs. T. Ball's grocery shop next door resulted in two deaths one being their daughter Barbara Ball. Two caretakers at the school escaped unhurt.

The greatest damage of this raid was in Duke Street and Foss Street clearly seen in the following pictures. Rundalls, the grocer, the adjacent butcher's shop, Rudd Prynns, outfitters, the Midland Bank and a drapery shop butting onto the Butterwalk were all destroyed with the tudor house in Foss Street left in such a condition that it had to be demolished. There were many miraculous escapes but the deaths were high as listed on page 24. Many nearby buildings were also damaged.

Within minutes of the dust settling the Civil Defences went into action with the mayor, Alderman W. Row, throwing himself into the efforts together with the A.R.P., troops stationed in Dartmouth, fire fighters, ambulances, First Aid parties and many others. The work went on through Saturday night under light of arc lamps which at one time were switched off because of a raid on Torquay. By late Sunday all the trapped persons had been rescued, the roads were being cleared and dangerous parts of the buildings torn down. The town had suffered its worst raid but was ready for business on the Monday.

Clearing up along Duke Street

This view of the extensive bomb damage of 13th February, 1943, along Duke Street shows the sites of the corner fruit shop of Rundals, Howe's, the gents tailors, and part of the Midland Bank site. Foss Street runs from the left and the damaged wooden framed building was considered too unsafe and later demolished. See F.C. Holwill's view of Foss Street taken in the late 1930's.

Rescue Work on the site of the Midland Bank

This photograph was taken within hours of the bank being destroyed late Saturday morning, 13th February, 1943. Two people were killed in it, the manager, Mr. Ronald Hocken, and a customer Mr. Ernest Pook. The Dartmouth rescue workers are hard at work; others are offering help standing in Duke Street in front of the shattered gent's tailor shop and the National Provincial Bank building.

Looking towards the Damaged Butterwalk

This view of Duke Street shows the blast damage to buildings close to the bombed Midland Bank, many being repaired later, two or three being taken down and rebuilt. This photograph was probably taken a week or so after 13th February; the sites are being cleared and Duke Street made accessible. Note the iron water pipe, a common sight in many towns when normal water supplies were disrupted to homes.

Looking towards Flavel Hall

This view of the extensive damage from the raid on 13th February, 1943, was probably taken from an upper window of the National Provincial Bank in Duke Street. A small notice in the foreground reads that the Midland Bank is working at Dawes, The Quay; Flavel Hall lost all its windows, the roof is severely damaged and another building in Foss Street is covered with a tarpaulin sheet.

Pre-War Foss Street

The end of Foss Street in the late 1930s showing the Tudor building and the corner shop destroyed in the blitz of 1943.

List of Casualties

Details taken from the records of the War Graves Commission which are at variance with the list from Noss Works on the board in their offices.

Casualties in the Raids on Dartmouth

At Noss Works on 18 September 1942:
Ash, John Richard, age 21, Home Guard, of Brixham
Lewis, Walter, age 40, of Dartmouth
Putt, Hubert William, age 37, Home Guard, of Townstall
Veale, Samuel James, age 21, Home Guard, of Dartmouth
Weaver, Hazel Joan, age 20, W.V.S., of Dartmouth

On River Dart on 18 September 1942:
Horne, John Henry, age 60, of Dartmouth
Northmore, John David, age 70, of Dartmouth
Pedwell, George Frederick, age 60, of Dartmouth
Saunders, George Edward, age 43, of Dartmouth

At Dartmouth on 13 February 1943:
Abrahams, Mabel, age 36, of Torquay, at 20 Duke Street
Andrew, Dorothy Irene, age 22, of Dartmouth, at 20 Duke Street
Ash, David, age 13, of Dartmouth, at Higher Street
Ball, Barbara Joan, age 20, W.V.S., of Dartmouth, at 20 Higher Street
Ball, Mary Elizabeth, age 52, of Dartmouth, at 20 Duke Street
Chapman, Jessie Rebecca, age 36, W.V.S., of Blackawton, at Howes shop, Duke S
Coles, Harriet Kate, age 61, W.V.S., of Dartmouth, at 8 Higherside
Dodridge, Marjory Louise, age 26, of Dartmouth, at 16 Duke Street
Grant, Caroline Agnes, age 50, of Dartmouth, at Higher Street
Heard, Frederick Dennis, age 2, of Dartmouth, at Eastmans, Duke Street
Hockin, Ronald, age 37, special constable, of St. Austell, at Midland Bank
Joseph, John William, age 17, Home Guard, of Kingswear, at Midland Bank
Plummer, Beatrice, age 48, of Dartmouth, at 20 Duke Street
Plummer, Trevor Lewis, age 4, of Dartmouth, at 20 Duke Street
Pook, Ernest James, age 60, of Dartmouth, at Midland Bank, Duke Street

At Board School Steps on 5 September 1943:
Davey, Harold, age 59, of 5 Board School Steps
 Killed by falling roof tiles hit by shell from ship on the river

At Halwell Road on 26 July 1944:
Harford, Henry John, age 33, N.F.S., of Thornton Heath, Surrey

U.S. NAVAL ADVANCED AMPHIBIOUS BASE, DARTMOUTH, DEVON
1943-44

It was 0530 on the morning of 22nd November, 1943, when the Advance party of NARO 114 consisting of some 150 men arrived in the Kingswear railroad station. It was cold and wet, typical of the mornings that this little ragged crew was to encounter for the next four months. And this little crew was really ragged, spiritually as well as physically. An overnight train ride from Scotland on a heatless train with only K rations for sustenance had augmented the gnawing nostalgia that ordinarily besets men far away from home.

A railway agent, upon being questioned, revealed that Dartmouth was across the river from Kingswear. But the Army trucks which finally rolled down the hill to pick up the unit didn't cross the river at all but turned back up winding, hilly, muddy roads through the English countryside to a lonely spot some ten miles from the railroad station. In the distance, joined to the main road by a cow path some 200 yards long and ten inches deep in mud, stood *Sandridge Park*, the first English home of NARO 114.

From the outside, *Sandridge Park* resembled a moderate-sized Hollywood version of an English castle. To say that it did not possess all of the modern conveniences would be an understatement; even its medieval conveniences were inoperable. Sandridge possessed nothing but space and a great deal of its space was not properly surrounded by the requisite number of walls. Sandridge was dirty and muddy and drafty and inadequate, but the NARO 114 unit settled down and began its existence in England there. Later Sandridge was destined to become a 1,000-man camp complete with Quonsett huts and powerful electric lights which put to shame the four invaluable kerosene lanterns which were the only means of illumination when the unit first arrived.

For the first month the advance nucleus of the NARO unit spent its time taking care of itself — and tolerating Sandridge. Trials were plentiful. The ancient English ranges in the galley had to be fired at least eight hours prior to the time that they would be used; the only means of heating the house, fireplaces, constituted a fire menace; there was no light in the house and no flash lights available; there was no means of transportation between Sandridge and the *Waddeton Court*, the officers' quarters two miles away. And the oppressive English weather was ever present adding to these discomforts.

Preparing for an Assault Exercise at Slapton

American army and naval personnel are checking equipment and vehicles on board this Landing Craft Tank 975 assisted by a Royal Naval personnel in the foreground. This was one of many amphibious craft assembling for the sea and landing exercise in Start Bay in April, 1944. The Dartmouth estuary is immediately behind the LCTs.

US 47 Landing Ship Tank

These ships were able to cross the sea at a convoy speed of 10 knots loaded with heavy vehicles and tanks and are seen here returning from one of the full scale exercises in the Slapton area. The port of Dartmouth was at its military height in the Spring of 1944 with many ships and amphibious vehicles filling almost the whole of the Dart estuary and land.

Then other pieces of English property were acquired as USNAAB Dartmouth began to expand, and to come to life as an institution. There was *Maypoole*, a magnificent two-storey house overlooking the river Dart; *Hunter's Lodge*, also overlooking the Dart; and *Greenway*, Agatha Christie's former home. All of these English homes tucked away miles apart in the English countryside were destined to become Staff Headquarters for LCI(L), LST, and LCT Flotillas. They were used by base personnel pending the time when the Royal Naval College in Dartmouth, across the river Dart, would become available for occupancy. The fact that these quarters were so far apart made transportation a prime problem. Effective administration was impossible under these conditions. Still there was little to administer at this time. NARO 114 was still doing little more than tending its own needs and carrying on very preliminary organization for the part it was to play in the invasion of Europe. This role did not begin to take real shape until the unit moved into the *Royal Naval College* in Dartmouth on 27th December, 1943.

The unit moved in hot on the heels of the Royal Marines who had been using the college as a Combined Operations training centre. So hot on their heels indeed that on the day of the move, the English had lunch in the college and the U.S. Navy took over for evening chow. The waterfront section of Dartmouth, which was set up with shops and was to be used as the repair division of NARO 114, had already been invaded when stores had arrived unexpectedly from a ship docked in Plymouth and the supply officer had been forced to off load them in an area which was still being used by the British.

Many of the problems that had been encountered at Sandridge recurred at the college. The Royal Naval College was a huge building situated high on a hill overlooking the river Dart. As "the Annapolis of England" it had accumulated quite a few traditions and customs, none of which made much of an impression on the arriving Yanks. They were more interested in plumbing and heat and other comfort-giving facilities. None of these had been maintained as astutely as the aforementioned customs and traditions. To most of the NARO 114 unit the inside of the Royal Naval College never ceased to appear cold and drab and unfriendly, although its plumbing and heating underwent agreeable transformation at the hands of the CB's. Extensive cleaning and repair operations were necessary to make it liveable. The galley ranges again proved difficult, and there was much trouble in regard to the allocation of space since most of the rooms, which had formerly been used as classrooms, had to be converted to living quarters.

Half-opened crates filled the austere halls of the College which were now alive with the raucous voices of sailors seeking "sacks". Officers cast avaricious eyes at the choice rooms, hoping to acquire them as quarters or office space. Housekeeping gear and bunks and toilet paper and other assorted essentials were at a premium. The Royal Marines had not been careless in leaving supplies behind. Each of the Marines had carried with him in addition to his full pack, a light bulb snatched from one of the various chandeliers of the college. Many of the British officials were reluctant to leave the college. One Royal Navy Commander requested quarters from the C.O. and when this was denied insisted on maintaining his office space for another month or so — then moved a cot into his office and slept there for almost a month.

The supplies which came over from the United States at this time as a part of the original allowance list did not help much. Eighty-two hundred-pound concrete sinkers, yards of mosquito netting and tons of hut material were of little use in this renovation. They were intended for a camp unit in a different climate. Most of the housekeeping stores did not arrive until long after essential items had already been procured from British sources. Many humorous incidents occurred in the course of this procurement. English and American terminologies were so different that storekeepers began to wonder if, after all, the two tongues were the same; the English had nothing corresponding to a swab, the basic American Navy cleaning tool (these were later made laboriously by cutting strips of canvas and securing them to the end of a broom stick).

A Casualty of a German Night Attack

This severely damaged Landing Ship Tank US 289 has arrived back in Dartmouth on the morning of 28th April, 1944. She was hit at 02.30 hours while on exercise in Start Bay by high speed German S-boats, six leaving Cherbourg undercover of darkness and slipping between a line of ships guarding the exercise area. The S-boats were armed with 20mm cannon and could reach a top speed of 35 knots.

Preparations for D-Day, 6th June 1944: Soon, however, USNAAB was on its feet and beginning its job as a part of the invasion force. The main function of the base was repairing ships and that it did with gusto. All types of craft were repaired — LST's, LCI(L)'s, LCT's, LCM's and LCV(P)'s. From the first day of operation to D-day, 1,400 landing craft were serviced by the E-6 Repair Unit. During this time the complement of this unit was increased from 288 to 550 men. The bulk of DD Ramp Extensions and Mulock Ramp Extensions were installed on LCT's by this unit. During the two weeks prior to D-day, 44 H.M. LCT's and 45 U.S. LCT's were repaired, in addition to the normal maintenance programme on LCI(L)'s, LCM's and LCV(P)'s. From D-day to D 30, one and one-half landing craft per day, damaged by battle or storm on the far shore, were repaired. In the second week of August, 1944, in addition to the slipways at Waddeton, a 475-ton pontoon drydock was set up and the complement of the Repair Unit expanded to 725 men. Up to and including 1st October, 1944, approximately 2,000 landing craft were repaired by USNAAB, Dartmouth, including PC's and SC's.

Another important function was supply. All of the craft which came to Dartmouth for repairs or on operations obtained supplies from the base, everything from needles to anchors. Provisions, canteen items, and clothing and small stores were provided for craft. And every request was a priority request. In the days just before and after D-day, USNAAB acted as Supply Base for 21 LST's, 17 LCI(L)'s, 63 LCT's, 50 LCM's, 35 LCV(P)'s, six AM's, five LCT(R)'s, four SC's, six PC's, four LCC's, 26 LCT(A)'s, ten Rhino Barges and three PT's.

As D-day drew near the operations function became more and more important. Pre-invasion exercises and manoeuvres had been plentiful. Practice loadings were made constantly at the hards in the Dartmouth area. (It was during these practice exercises that the Operations Department, USNAAB, Dartmouth, developed a pontoon loading ramp, built from Rhino Barge pontoons which permitted vehicles to be loaded aboard an LST without danger of grounding the ship). The narrow English roads became periodic hosts to long strings of Army tanks and other armoured vehicles. Driving along the roads at night one could see long convoys of such vehicles pulled up to the side of the road, each piece of equipment covered with camouflage netting. The English people had become accustomed to the noisy squeak and rumble of mechanized equipment on the march.

And with the increase of operations came an increase in personnel. Men flowed into the college from all directions; Army units of various types, British Liaison groups, war correspondents, high ranking Army and Navy officials on observation tours and a number of enlisted personnel to supplement the hard-pressed base facilities. The college was filled to capacity and a tent city was set up. A second tent city was later established at Sandridge. Soon more than 4,000 Navy men were being quartered ashore in the Dartmouth area and every section of the base was working overtime. Personnel in the First Lieutenant's office were darting around like the proverbial decapitated chickens trying to create more space of which there was none, in which to put additional bunks which were unavailable.

The Welfare and Recreation department was struggling with the problem of entertaining 4,000 men who were hard at work and under the rigid restrictions of high security. Communication was badly in need of more telephone operators and more signalmen. And the Personnel office, was coping with long sailing lists, attempting to keep an accurate record of personnel involved in the invasion. At this point, USNAAB, Dartmouth, ran 12 messes, carried the pay accounts of more than 4,000 men, operated five canteens, while drafts of men arrived and departed 24 hours a day. Base personnel swelled to more than 2,000 and still there were not enough men to do what had to be done in the time alloted. Housing and messing facilities were established at Brixham and Torquay, where additional loading hards were situated, and crews to man the hards were selected from base personnel.

D-Day Arrives, 6th June, 1944: Finally the great day came. Speculation as to the date of D-day had run high and the crews which left the college to man the hards at Brixham and Torquay on 1st June were not at all sure that they were not taking part in another "Dry Run". Once again, loading took place in much the same fashion as in the pre-invasion exercises. Troops filled the narrow English roads leading down to the loading hards. The cleats of caterpillar tractors bit deep into the English soil. Huge modern tanks rumbled down roads that had been built in the seventeenth century. Many of them carried bouquets of flowers peeping forth from their gun barrels. CB's gathered up their gas masks and helmets and boarded the Rhino Barges which they had built from pontoons.

Loading went on steadily for three days with no rest for anyone. Each craft was scheduled to be loaded at a certain time and the schedule must be met. In the Dartmouth area three large transports and 15 LCI(L)'s were loaded with troops and 20 LST's and 145 LCT's were loaded with mechanized equipment and troops. Then, after three days, loading was completed on schedule and there was time again to speculate as to whether it was the "real thing" this time. Speculation in the affirmative was dampened by the storm which swept England on the night of 4th June. But when the hard crews wakened on the morning of 6th June from their first real sleep in a week, the radio greeted them with the news that this was the real thing after all, that this time they had loaded for a purpose.

Closing Down Operations: After D-day the importance of USNAAB, Dartmouth, as a base began to wane. It was too far west to be used regularly in the "build-up" between England and France. For the same reason it received few casualties. It became instead the headquarters for an escort control group of SC's and PC's and home port for a number of Army tugs which towed barges to the far shore. It also began to act as a receiving station. A draft of Beach Battalion and Gunfire Support personnel was assembled there for shipment back to the United States, and it was used as a pool for men who were on their way to the far shore. Sandridge Park became a rest camp and recreation centre for personnel returning from France. The LCI(L) Flotilla which had occupied Maypoole returned to the States.

Maypoole, Greenway, Hunter's Lodge and *Waddeton Court* were closed up and turned back to the British. Only the two larger buildings, the college and *Sandridge Park* remained of USNAAB, Dartmouth. Just as it had expanded quickly, the base, now contracted hurriedly, retaining just enough of its former self to see safely the men of the Fleet whose needs it had tended off to other parts of the world   *Official report from Washington, U.S.A.*

US541 and US209 LSTs

Another scene of the very busy Dartmouth estuary in the build up to the Normandy Landings on the 6th June, 1944. Ambulance jeeps are disembarking from the Landing Ship Tank onto a "hard" running up the North Embankment. Note the steaming tug in the background.

Awaiting Orders

The U.S.S. Landing Craft Tank 47 and a L.S.T. wait for the invasion order fully armed and loaded with vehicles on the river Dart on 2nd June, 1944.

Bringing the Casualties Ashore

The LST 298 is docked by the North Embankment and casualties of the night attack by S-Boats are carried along the catwalk from the deck of the ship and from its hold.

Rhino Barge

These heavily loaded self propelled rafts were made up of steel pontoons the largest weighing 400 tons, 45 ft. wide by 175 ft. in length. Unstable in rough seas many were lost in the gales of early June, 1944.

Landing Ship Tank 289

A close view of the seriously damaged 40mm single gun platform hanging vertical above the damaged ship's line. Note the coal gantry in the background.

A Sad Sight

A few boats mill around the stern damaged LST on 28th April, 1944, but work must start to repair the twisted metal and make this Landing Ship Tank seaworthy as soon as possible.

Side View of LST 289

Now safety moored alongside the North Embankment white capped U.S. sailors look aghast at the damage inflicted by the night attack by German S-boats from Cherbourg equipped with torpedos.

Motorised Vehicles

The capacity of the Landing Ship Tanks was large for carrying a variety of military vehicles and tanks. U.S.47 is disembarking its hold of vehicles while on deck gunners man a gun should enemy planes attack.

1st June 1944

Troops and Howitzers are here being guided into Landing Craft Tank 821 at Dartmouth in readiness for the Normandy Invasion although almost all troops were unaware of actual plans or dates for this historic onslaught into German held France.

1st June 1944

A U.S. Army M.7 self-propelled 105mm Howitzer from battery "B", 42nd Field Artillery, awaiting to go aboard a Landing Craft Tank for the Normandy Invasion.

Operation Duck

Embarking for the first large scale landing at Slapton on 27th to 31st March, 1943, from a concrete landing ramp by the Higher Ferry. Sherman tanks are coming aboard an LTC (landing tank craft) waterproofed for the sea crossing.

Higher Ferry Embarkation Point

Troops have embarked in the nearest of the Landing Craft Vehicle and Personnel from "C" position and others are moving from "D" position on the hard assisted by U.S. Naval personnel on both amphibious vehicles. *Operation Duck* preparations.

In Full Battle Dress

U.S. Army forces in full battle order await on a "hard" for landing craft to take them out to sea in preparation for the landing exercise at Slapton from 27th to 31st March, 1944.

On Route for Normandy

Although this is a general view of many U.S. ships making their way to Start Bay for one of the exercises, it does give a good idea of what the general scene must have been when 485 ships left the safety of Dartmouth for the Channel crossing to storm the Normandy beaches on 6th June, 1944.

"For Freedom"

This large stone commemorative plaque records that 485 ships of the U.S. Navy left Dartmouth for France in that eventful month of June, 1944. It is situated on the south part of North Embankment.

> **FOR FREEDOM**
>
> THIS MEMORIAL WAS ERECTED TO COMMEMORATE THE SAILING FROM THIS PORT ON 3RD JUNE 1944 OF AN AMPHIBIOUS FORCE OF 485 SHIPS OF THE UNITED STATES NAVY TO TAKE PART IN THE INVASION OF NORMANDY AND THE LIBERATION OF THE OPPRESSED COUNTRIES OF NORTH WEST EUROPE.
>
> I THE LORD WILL HOLD THY RIGHT HAND, SAYING UNTO THEE. "FEAR NOT; I WILL HELP THEE."
>
> ISA. XL. 13.
>
> UNVEILED ON JULY 12TH 1954, BY H.R.H. THE DUKE OF EDINBURGH.

Landing Craft Abbreviations
L.C.I.(L): Landing Craft Infantry (Large)
L.S.T.: Landing Ship Tank
L.C.T.: Landing Craft Tank
L.C.A.: Landing Craft Assault
L.C.V.P.: Landing Craft Vehicle and Personnel
L.C.M.: Landing Craft Mechanical

Wartime Reports for 1945

Dartmouth Man Missing

News was received by Mr. and Mr. H. Maunder of 199 Victoria Road last week that their son Ft.Sgt.Eng. Frederick Hancock has been reported missing over Germany on the night of 2/3 February. His aircraft failed to return. *February 1945*

Kingswear N.F.S. Stand down

Members of this part-time unit have received orders to stand down. They held a dance in the Kingswear Hall last Friday in aid of the Welfare Fund. Fireman A.V. Hurt was M.C. Door stewards were Fireman Thyer, Knapman and Thyer, junior. *March 1945*

Home Guard Stand down Dinner

This was held in Dawe's Criterion restaurant by members of No.2 platoon "D" company. Major H.C. Lloyd, Captain J.H. Hill, Lt. and Mrs. J. Lee and members and friends were in attendance. Lt. Hannaford was the platoon commander. *March 1945*

P.O.W. Feted at Open Air Dance

For four hours on Saturday evening amid flags and bunting a returned Dartmouth p.o.w. was entertained to an open air welcome home dance in Britannia Avenue, Townstal. Organised by Mrs. J.A. Newman, Mrs. Atkins and Mr. D. Atkins as M.C. Cake and wine were served to the former p.o.w. McCall from a heavily laden table. *June 1945*

Removal of Shelters begins in Schools

Morrison shelters are in the process of being removed from the Infants' and Girls' schools in Dartmouth. *August 1945*

Kingswear Bride of former P.O.W.

A prisoner of war for five years in Germany, Mr. J.R. Hearn of Above Town was married in St. Thomas a Becket Church, Kingswear, on Saturday to Miss Betty A. Wallace of Kingswear. *September 1945*

Town Honours the Mayor

In recognition of their work for Dartmouth during the past six years the Mayor and Mayoress, Alderman and Mrs. W.G. Row, were presented at a gathering in the Guildhall last night with a silver tea service to the purchase of which all sections of the community contributed. The tea service which had been on view in the window of R.J. Bennett, outfitter, on The Quay. The presentation comprises a George I tray, teapot, hot water jug, milk jug and sugar basin. The Mayor elect, councillor H.G. Middleton, presided. *November 1945*

Casualties at the Noss Shipyard

This commemorative stone stands at the entrance to Sandquay works and was erected in 1988 some forty-six years after the raid on Noss Works on the opposite side of the estuary. There a board records the memory of the following who died in the raid on 18th September, 1942. They are Frederick C. Adams, John R. Ash, David Bott, John G. C. Bustin, Rose A. Crang, Thomas Farr, Richard Franklin, Lionel E. Holden, Walter Lewis, George H. F. Little, Henry J. Luckhurst, John Martin, Sidney Pope, Ernest Poole, Hubert E. W. Putt, Ewart E. Trant, Nellie E. Trebilcock, Samuel J. Veale, Frederick Vickery and Hazel J. Weaver.

(Reuter's Telegram)

GERMANY HAS SURRENDERED

A SAN FRANCISCO message says that Germany has surrendered to the Allied Governments unconditionally.

An announcement is expected immediately.

A high American official said the surrender would presumably be made to General Eisenhower.

An announcement was expected at 16.00 E.W.T., but was delayed.

While he was not informed of all details, the surrender was made to the Three Powers.

Aircraft Crashes around Dartmouth

15th July 1940: A Hawker Hurricane fighter plane from R.A.F. Exeter attacked a low flying German Dornier over the Dart estuary without effect but in return was attacked itself close to the estuary and crashed into the sea near Eastern Black Rock.

22nd March 1943: A German Dornier 217 made a low level attack on Dartmouth crashing into the sea after receiving a hit from land defences.

23rd March 1943: A Folke-Wolf plane was shot down by an anti-aircraft battery and crashed near Strete killing the pilot.

15th May 1944: A Hurricane from R.A.F. Bolt Head hit a barrage balloon cable and crashed into fields now part of Archway Drive. All the crew and passengers were killed one being an Air Commodore who had made an inspection of R.A.F. Bolt Head the previous day.

WOMANS ROYAL NAVAL SERVICE

Members of this service were drafted into the Dartmouth area in 1942 first at the Royal Naval College then, as numbers increased, to various requisitioned houses and hotels affectionately known as *Wreneries*. These were Newcomen, officers' quarters, Mount Boone, from late 1943, Moorings and Broadstones, in the town, Manor House, Woodford and Devonia, overlooking the river, Warfleet and Derwent Lodge near the castle. The Mount, The Beacon and Inverdart at Kingswear. Sandridge Lodge, Greenway House and Hunter's Lodge were occupied with a skeleton staff up to D Day.

The R.N. College and annexes became H.M.S. *Effingham* where training took place and combined operations between services functioned. Their H.Q. was at H.M.S. *Cicala* the Royal Dart Hotel, where all the work was oversighted especially during the very hectic days prior to the Normandy Landings. At this time there were over 700 personnel in the area undertaking a wide variety of non-combatant duties from operating searchlights, aiming anti-aircraft guns, driving ambulances and other vehicles, telephonists and taking a thousand and one confidential maps and documents to units assembling for D Day. The work often took them to Plymouth, Teignmouth, Torquay and Brixham.

The girls in blue were a very familiar sight dashing around and manning launches on the river assisting in all manner of duties including helping in the air raids, providing comfort and support for the injured, refreshments and a host of other supporting work.

H.M.S. Cicala, Summer 1944

Staff of the confidential books office are grouped showing in the top row Wrens Brooks, Tebbuts, Sanders, Blackwell, Barrow, Hurford and Rule. In the front row are Petty Officer Blake, Second Officer Deran, Third Officer Charlton and Leading Wren Hole. The white lanyards denote boat's crew.

Group at the College

Seen here in 1943 are Leading Seaman Wright, O.D. Stocks, R.N., and three M/T Wrens Charlton, Blackborever and Du Plessis, O.D. Morley, R.N., and Mr. Herd who was then the College driver. Initially there were four W.R.N.S. and four men drivers increasing to six by 1944.

The War is Over!
VE HOW DARTMOUTH CELEBRATED VE

Great crowds of dancing, cheering townspeople, wearing national emblems, celebrated VE-Day in Dartmouth. As the bars of the National Anthem boomed over countless radios following the Prime Minister's historic broadcast announcing the victorious end of the war in Europe, church bells rang out in a wildly joyous peal, ships of every description in the river sounded sirens and hooters and even railway engines waiting to pull out from Kingswear Station joined their whistles to the mad medley of noise which met the long-awaited announcement.

Crowds in holiday mood thronged the embankments where many listened to the broadcast thanksgiving service relayed over the loudspeaker system of a U.S. warship moored alongside.

Every street in the town was gaily bedecked with great Union Jacks flapping in the breeze, flags of a score of Allied Nations and bunting of every colour and style. There has hardly been a window in the past week which has not been decorated.

Merriest Scene of All

Picturesque Bayard's Cove presented the merriest scene of all. The evening before, when news of the unconditional surrender of Germany was first received, housewives in the vicinity had got together and planned a party in the street.

Tables were set up and loaded with a great variety of good things and nearly 100 children, some of them from the furthest corners of the town, settled down to enjoy the party.

While they drank lemonade and tucked away sandwiches, cakes and buns, Mr. Bill Bellamy, with his accordion, and Mr. Bert Davey, led the crowd in singing some of the popular songs of both world wars.

Crowds continued to throng the streets until evening and smoke-bombs and fireworks were set off at intervals.

Every church in the town was crowded to the doors for the thanksgiving services, and later in the evening there was a great dancing throng around the Bandstand in Royal Avenue Gardens where Bill Fletcher's band provided the music, which they introduced with the national anthems of Russia, the United States and Great Britain.

Giant "V" Sign

Dancing ceased at 9 o'clock when the Mayor (Ald. W. G. Row), who was accompanied by the Mayoress, mounted the stand to announce that the King's speech to the nation was to be relayed.

The crowd afterwards sang the National Anthem and the Mayor led three cheers for Their Majesties.

Old favourites, such as the lancers, were the order of the evening and dancing continued until after black-out time. Even although the orders keeping curtains drawn on this part of the coast are still in operation searchlights from river-craft lit up the crowd and a giant "V" sign in multi-coloured lights flashed along the waterfront from a window in Lloyd's Bank Chambers.

Hotels and bars remained open until 11 p.m. and it was long after midnight before merry-makers cleared the streets. In several bars dances were in progress and American sailors entertained in one place.

Celebrations continued on the second day of the national holiday and the town was densely crowded in the evening when dancing in Royal Avenue Gardens again continued long after black-out time.

MESSAGE TO THE BROKEN-HEARTED

Bereaved Remembered Amid Rejoicing

Townspeople who were "breaking their hearts in secret for the loss of those who will never return" were remembered by Rev. A. J. Watts, Vicar of Dartmouth and Townstal, preaching at the principal thanksgiving service of the day held at St. Saviour's.

He was preaching on the words, "O give thanks unto the Lord," and declared, "It is with full hearts that we have come together in this holy place on this historic day which marks the end of so many years of slaughter. It is not, however, for many people, the end of sorrow and tears, for even as we meet here, some must be breaking their hearts in secret for the loss of those who will never return.

"Our hearts go out to them all. But it is right and proper that tonight we should show our gladness of heart in true merriment."

Spirit of Gladness

The merry bells, tumbling over each other for joy, he went on, the dancing in the gardens, were all in keeping with the spirit of gladness. They were glad, but that was not, by any means, all there was to it. They were there because they were not only glad but thankful, and thanksgiving was an essentially Godward activity.

It must not be a merely occasional thing, he stressed, an isolated parade, a momentary nod of acknowledgement. True Christian thanksgiving showed itself in a life of regular worship and prayer; and a nation whose people were a praying, worshipping people would have little need to fear the future, for they would begin by recognizing the world as God's world; they would plan according to the Divine Law, and by the strength of God's grace they would see it through.

The climax of the service was the singing by the congregation of the solemn "Te Deum."

The Climax

The Vicar was assisted by Mr. W. Parr Ferris, Vicar's Warden and M.C.; Mr. G. Crabb, thurifer; Mr. T. Densham, thurifer; and Messrs. D. Spencer and A. Holmes, acolytes. The organist was Dr. John Wray, M.A. F.R.C.O., of Paignton.

Part of a local newspaper report giving details of the VE celebrations.

Street Party

A typical scene all over Dartmouth and Kingswear as part of the celebrations for victory. Here Brian Penwill, Grandpie Vallance, holding a beer jug, and John Penwill are with neighbours at the rear of 40 Southwood Road a few days after Victory in Europe was announced on 8th May, 1945.

Celebration Parties

The first two pictures are at Brown Steps where Mrs. E. Williams, Mrs. F. Williams and Miss H. Hayman, whose small shop is on the right, organised the VE party for nearby children. Councillor Harold Adams is in attendance; recognised are Miss Rehburgh, Miss Hearn, Francis Preece, Kathleen Cole, Rose Pearce, Maud Brown, Mr. and Mrs. Kelland, who lived opposite the shop, Mrs. Humphreys, sat in chair, and Chrissie Hamlyn among others.

Gifts of sweets were given by Mr. L. Lucas, while fish and chips were supplied through Mrs. Perring. Mr. Poole also gave gifts to the children.

The bottom scene comes from Crowther's Hill, the group celebrating VJ day on 15th August, 1945. Recognised are Leonard Thorne, Fred Partridge, Bill Row, ex-mayor, Mrs. Partridge and Mr. Foley.

1945: VICTORY CELEBRATIONS AT DARTMOUTH AND KINGSWEAR

By the opening months of 1945 victory in Europe was at last in view with Allied Forces closing around Germany and Hitler's reign coming to an end. The German radio announced on 1st May, 1945, that Hitler was dead; his forces unconditionally surrendered and VE Day was announced for 8th May. Three months later Japan surrendered and VJ Day (Victory over Japan) was declared on 14th August, 1945.

The whole of the country went wild with celebrations and Dartmouth and Kingswear were no exception to the euphoria which swept across the land. The loss of relatives and friends, the return of injured personnel and the damage to property was part of the price for this victory.

The Mayor's tour first took in Ferndale Road where tea and games were taking place organised by Mr. and Mrs. L. Thorne, Mr. and Mrs. F. C. Sanders and Mrs. R. Widdicombe.

More than 80 children sat down to tea from the Avery's Meadow and Victoria Road area in the decorated playground of the Boys' Council School with Mr. E. Rees, headmaster, overlooking and listening to music. Mrs. L. Jago and others organised the eats while Mr. Jago and Mr. Packman made seesaws and swings for the children.

Next stop for the Mayor was at the tennis courts by the R.N. College the party taking place here for the Townstal area children. Here prizes were given and each child received a 1/-. Mr. J. Courtney's brass band led the singing and Mr. J. H. Cooper, Mrs. C. Heath and Mrs. F. Chope organised the party itself.

There was dancing in Britannia Avenue and an effigy of Hitler was burnt. About 90 children had eats organised by Mrs. D. Atkins, and Mrs. J. A. Newman under flags and bunting and entertainment was provided by Mr. John Foulkes on his accordion. Here the children received a bag of sweets and 6d.

The Drill Hall, Clarence Hill, was the scene of another party organised by Mrs. W. Callard with Mrs. W. J. Wotton, Mrs. W. Lee and Mrs. F. Anstey and games by Mr. T. G. Middleton and music by the Star Dance Band.

There was dancing in the Square with troops joining in and many other parties taking place in different localities. These were at Market Square, Above Town, South Ford school rooms and in the main street of Kingswear and in other places.

MAYOR'S TOUR

Celebration of the most glorious victory in the nation's history continued over the week-end in Dartmouth with dancing in the streets, bonfires, street parties in many parts of the town and an impressive demonstration, culminating in a service of thanksgiving, to end it all on Sunday.

In the blazing sunshine of Saturday the Mayor (Ald. W. G. Row), attired in his robes and wearing full regalia, accompanied by the Mayoress, the Deputy Mayor and Mayoress (Councillor and Mrs. H. G. Middleton), Inspector P. Gould, and Sergeant T. Badcock, toured the town.

Everywhere the Mayor and Mayoress and party were received with cheers and the singing of "For He's a Jolly Good Fellow." Excited children at street parties watched eagerly the approach of his gaily be-flagged car.

At each stop he paid tribute to the parents who had arranged the parties for the children. It was an important day in their lives, he said, and there would probably never be another quite like it. It was his hope, however, that something on an even more impressive scale might be arranged when the Japanese were also beaten.

He urged them to remember the occasion and always try to be happy together: The splendid co-operation between neighbours he thought augured well for the future.

VICTORY PARTIES IN THE STREETS

More Celebrations

Pamela Lake, the Misses Vintons and Mrs. M. Penwill have been recognised in this party also held in the Southwood Road area. Streets were bedecked with flags, tables arranged along roads and music and dancing made up part of the many events taking place in Dartmouth and Kingswear after five years of anxiety, toil, damaged property, loss of relatives and friends and the constant threat of attack by air or sea.

Dartmouth Honours its Mayor

Alderman and Mrs. W. G. Row are seen here receiving a silver tea service in recognition of their contribution to the town during the war years. The presentation took place in the Guildhall on 10th November, 1945. The Mayor elect, H. G. Middleton, presided. T. Wilton made the presentation watched by Alec Philip on the left. The tea service was bought through public subscription.

South Town in the 1940s

This wartime view shows part of Dartmouth's waterfront with the Yacht Hotel as it was before the bomb damage to the large wall and building rendering it uninhabitable. Many of the other buildings were requisitioned by the military. Laver's boatyard is on the right one of many yards working during that decade.

Warship Week, May, 1944

It was appropriate for Earl Mount Batten to open this fund raising week in Dartmouth while on a visit to the Royal Naval College. The mayor with the two maces on the table is presiding on the stage of the Guildhall. Also in attendance are two officers from the college; those on the right have not been recognised.

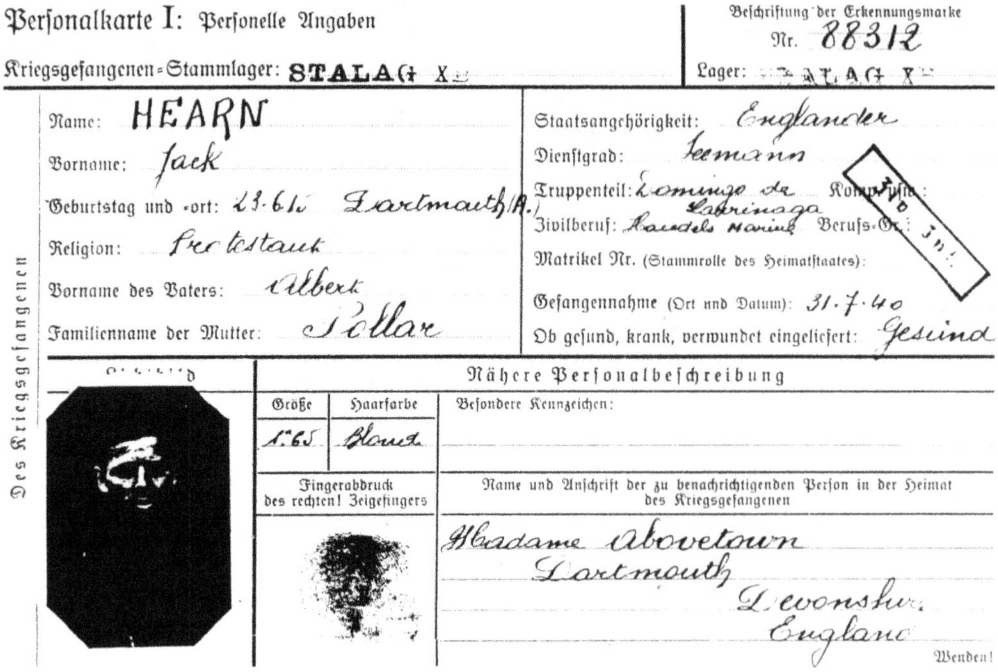

Wartime Memories

Jack Hearn's prisoner of war document issued to him in Stalag Camp is reproduced here. He spent most of the war in this camp which has featured in some films. Corrugated paper according to this local advertisement was the best material for the perfect blackout and those wishing to have a Morrison shelter would have had to respond to the notice of July, 1942. The familiar identity card had to be carried at all times and many people can remember being asked to show theirs.

FOR

The Perfect Black=out

USE

CORRUGATED PAPER

NOW ON SALE

AT

CRANFORD'S

4d. per yard or 5/6 per roll

PUBLIC NOTICES.

BOROUGH OF DARTMOUTH

Morrison Indoor Shelters— Free Supply and Purchase

THE Corporation give notice that a number of the above shelters will be available shortly.

Shelters will be supplied free to applicants who are mainly dependent on earnings (or pension) not exceeding £350 a year. (If there are more than two children of school age in the household this limit may be increased by £50 for each child in excess of two). Any other person may purchase a shelter for £7 each which must be paid at the time of application.

Applications for shelters must be made on forms which can be obtained from the undersigned, and they will be dealt with strictly in the order in which they are received. Persons making application for forms by post must state whether they are entitled to a shelter free or wish to purchase one, and must include an addressed envelope stamped with a one penny stamp. If completed forms are sent through the post the envelopes must be sealed and bear a 2½d. stamp.

The shelters are of table form, 6ft. 6in. by 4ft. 0in. by approximately 2ft. 5in. high and are designed for erection on the ground floor of a house and are a danger if used on any other floor. They are intended for houses of not more than three floors (including the basement, if any) and will not be supplied for larger premises.— H. D. P. BOTT, Town Clerk, Guildhall, Dartmouth, 2nd July, 1942.

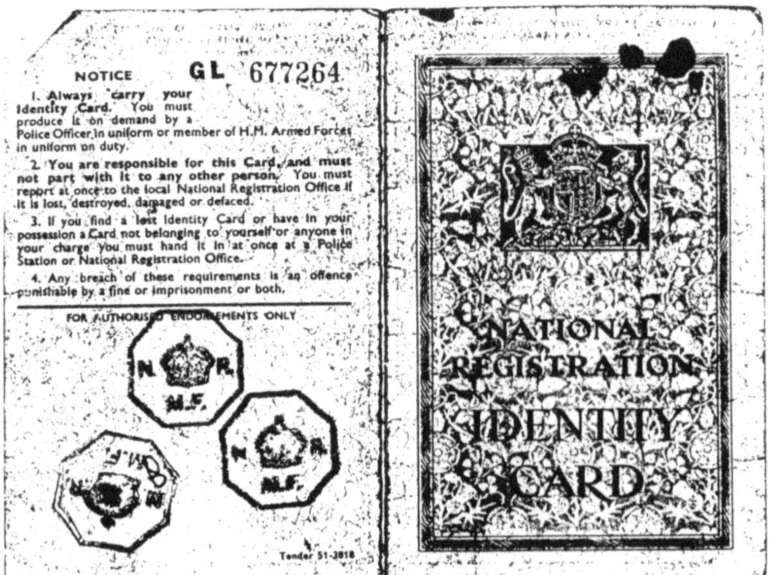

Arthur L. Clamp – the man behind the books

Arthur Leslie Clamp was a man of boundless energy with a passion for helping others, particularly through his love of history. A printer by trade, he started his career in a printing company before moving his family from Exeter to Plymouth to teach at the Plymouth College of Art and Design, where he eventually became the Head of the Printing Department.

A Devoted Family Man

Arthur with his five children.

Despite his love of teaching, Arthur prioritised his family, always making it home by 5:30pm for tea. He and his wife, Rosemary, raised five children: Susan, Angela, Elizabeth, David, and Steven. Arthur would often combine his love of family and history by taking his children on Sunday walks, encouraging them to appreciate historical monuments by taking photos or making crayon rubbings of gravestones for his books. The family home at 203 Elburton Road was a hub of activity, with a large garden, featuring a two-storey fort and a makeshift swimming pool.

A Lifelong Learner and Adventurer

Arthur's thirst for knowledge extended beyond history to a deep curiosity about the world. He was passionate about exploring different cultures, traditions, and cuisines, often taking advantage of his long summer holidays as a teacher to travel to places like India, Russia, South America, the middle east and the USA, sometimes bringing one of his children along. This adventurous spirit even influenced his home life, as seen by the short-lived family tradition of steam-cooking vegetables after a trip to Iceland.

History is a prominent feature of family days out

Community and Philanthropic Spirit

His commitment to serving others was evident in his long-standing involvement with the Elburton Methodist Church. He was the Sunday School Superintendent for over 15 years and served as the editor of the wider church's monthly newsletter, "The Link," for a similar duration. After Rosemary's very sad passing, Arthur later remarried and, following a chance encounter with a professor from India, established a connection with a missionary school in Chennai. Together with his new wife, Christine, he co-founded a "Sponsor a Child's Education" program that continues to this day.

*Pictured left – The cover of 'The Link' complete
with hand drawn sketches of each church by Angela
Below right – Arthur Clamp promoting his latest book
Below left – Arthur at home with his first wife, Rosemary
Below centre – Arthur on holiday with his second wife,
Christine*

A Legacy of Learning and Positivity

Arthur's greatest passion was history, which he brought to life through tireless research, documentation, and the many books he authored. He was driven by a need to "never be stuck in a rut," constantly seeking new experiences, meeting new people, and expanding his knowledge. With a positive attitude and a great sense of humour, he was always ready to help others, leaving a lasting impact on his family and community. His children, Susan, Angela, Elizabeth, David, and Steven, remember him with love and gratitude.

David Clamp, 2025

A Legacy of Local History

Below is the story of how Arthur L Clamp began writing books, in his own words, drafted shortly before he passed away in 2001. I have only made minor alterations to this text, correcting grammatical errors that he did not survive to correct himself. When I first discovered this text, I was shocked to see my name mentioned. It seems that, unbeknownst to me, I shared my first PC with him. I suspect he used it during the day when I was at school, although I do have one memory of sitting with him and showing him how it worked. It has been a pleasure to pick up where he left off and see his books republished and redistributed, and to know that I was part of the story, even back then. It was also fascinating to discover that his pricing structure matches the way I have tried to price the books, with a third going to local sellers and the rest covering printing costs with a little left over for my expenses.

I am his eldest grandson, and it is a privilege to curate his legacy, which we are calling 'The Clamp Collection'. The very last line of the text originally reads "The following pages list all the titles." Sadly, that page is missing and we have no record of all the books he published and knowing that some of those were researched by other authors makes the process of finding them even harder. I look forward to one day completing the collection and seeing them all available again. And maybe, one day, I'll even start writing my own to add to the series. For now, here is his story in his own words.

Steven Gibson, 2025

Writing and Publishing Booklets on Local Topics and Areas

I started this interest in either 1968 or 1969 when living in Woodford. I had by these dates established the Department of Printing and I think I must have been looking for something different to do. The first titles were of A5 size proofed from type set at Clarke, Doble and Brendon, Ltd., Plymouth printers, and then made up into pages and printed at Sawtell and Neilson, Ltd., Totnes.

Then began a slow process of getting them out to shops, etc. which proved to be more time consuming and difficult than actually researching, writing and getting the books into print. However, I persisted and opened a business account with Barclays Bank on the Broadway. I was advised to give it a title so I called it "Westway Publications". There came along another problem, one of storage of paper and finished books which was solved when the family moved to Elburton in 1970.

I changed the printer to Penwell, Ltd., Callington, Cornwall, as he was then just setting up himself and his prices seemed very reasonable. I did not get any of the printers to make up the complete books. I hand folded the flat printed sheets, stitched the books on a small manual table stitcher and trimmed them in a small hand turned guillotine which I bought from someone in Penzance for £40. It was brought up in a van.

The trouble and time going to and fro to Callington was too much so I transferred the printing to PDS Printers, Prince Rock, Plymouth, and I have been with them ever since. Now they are at Plympton which is easy to reach and they fold the flat sheets which was turning out to be a long chore which only saved a small part of the printing costs.

All my first titles were written by myself. I took the photographs and developed them in the loft of the house, the type was set by now on a computer situated in the house at Elburton from which I had collected photographic lengths of text to cut up and law down as pages.

At some point I decided that I would do my own film processing of lith film so I bought a large second hand process camera from Kingsbridge and learnt through trial and error to make line negatives of the text and halftone negatives of the illustrations which proved more difficult than I anticipated. The main problem was trying to keep the developer in the large dish at the correct temperature as any change would affect the developing time. I replaced this old camera with a brand new one bought from Croydon, Surrey, costing £900. This has turned out to be a great asset cutting out an expensive part of the printer's costs and one crucial aspect of the work which I could control.

By the middle 1970s there were many outlets I had contacted in Plymouth, up to Dartmoor, Exeter, around to Torbay, Totnes, Dartmouth and the South Hams. The market for local books was much greater than I had first thought and through getting to know many local people undertaking research themselves had the chance to help and make up books for other people who had in most instances, got together a collection of photographs with some text in a rather muddled way. Through my experience in print I was able to shape up their work and get it into print and in every case I had to pay the printer and let the person have the royalties. In the majority of titles produced in this manner this was another way of producing titles and it did give some profit to my work. However, I must say that in a few cases I lost out by either the other person getting the numbers wrong, not returning any monies from stock I delivered or they thought that more of their books should have been sold.

The print run was usually 1,000 copies and from time to time I have had reprints of 250 copies. It took about ten years to clear the first print run so I always had large stocks in the garage, workshop, etc. The numbers sold during the early years was about 7,000 copies a year increasing to around 9,000 copies and for the whole of the enterprise about 500,000 have been sold. The booklets have become part of the local scene and many people collect them, shops regularly order copies and I go around certain areas month by month restocking or replacing titles as necessary.

During the past year or so I have started setting the text on a Packard Bell PC, something which I should have done some years back. I share it with Steven Gibson, my grandson. There appears to be no end to the market for local books, but I could not earn a regular income because of the long time it takes to sell stock.

However, now exceeding 100 titles made up mainly of A4 twenty-four page booklets, some folded guides, with selling prices set with a third going to the shop which is the trade custom, the original idea has been quite successful and could go on for ever.

Apart from monetary benefits, however spasmodically these might be, I have learnt a lot myself, met many interesting people and have become part of the local scene with requests to give talks and to advise people about getting into print.

Arthur L Clamp, 2001

This newspaper article, published by the Evening Herald on 17th August 2001, forms a good record of his life. Just as he encourages us to learn more about local history, we encourage you to learn a little about him. For that reason, we have included these pages at the back of all the most recently republished books, in honour of his memory and recognition of his contribution to the community.

www.ingramcontent.com/pod-product-compliance
Lightning Source LLC
Chambersburg PA
CBHW061403070526
44584CB00031B/4150